RACEHORSE

The complete guide to the world of horse racing

RACEHORSE

The complete guide to the world of horse racing

ELWYN HARTLEY EDWARDS

written by Elwyn Hartley Edwards
additional writing by Debby Sly

Produced for the AA by

 studio **cactus** ltd Ⓒ

12 SOUTHGATE STREET WINCHESTER HAMPSHIRE SO23 9DZ UK
TEL 00 44 1962 878600 EMAIL MAIL@STUDIOCACTUS.CO.UK WEBSITE WWW.STUDIOCACTUS.CO.UK

design Sharon Rudd
editorial Jennifer Close
picture research Sian Lloyd

© AA Media Limited 2008

Colour separation by MRM Graphics Ltd,
Winslow

Printed and bound by C & C Offset
Printing Co Ltd, China

A CIP catalogue record for this book is
available from the British Library.

ISBN 978-0-7495-6744-6
ISBN 978-0-7495-6782-8 (SS)

Revised 2009
Reprinted Nov 2010

Published by AA Publishing, a trading name
of AA Media Limited, whose registered office
is Fanum House, Basing View, Basingstoke,
Hampshire RG21 4EA. Registered no.
06112600.

A04496

CONTENTS

FOREWORD

I am honoured to be asked to write the foreword for this lavish book, which celebrates the world of racing and the magnificent Thoroughbreds that grace our racecourses. The book examines the origins and traditions of our sport and tracks the progress that has been made for racing to become a multi-billion-pound business that holds its own on the world stage. As we move forward with the times, I believe that racing needs to constantly evolve, both nurturing the old and embracing the new.

Ever since I stood in the stands watching my Father, George, riding around the tracks in the north of Ireland, I was captivated by the speed, power and nobility of the horse. As a result, all I ever wanted to be was a jockey. With a lot of luck, a small amount of talent and with a bit of hard work thrown in, I realised this dream and just a few years later found myself at the centre of this intriguing world, the 'Sport of Kings' – with all its colour, drama and characters.

Like myself, Elwyn received his vision and his love for the horse from his Father and this book is not only a celebration of this world, but also of a very full life spent at the heart of racing.

RICHARD DUNWOODY MBE

Throughout his life Elwyn Hartley Edwards was first and foremost a horseman. Editor of Riding *magazine for 18 years, consultant editor of* Horse & Hound, *he was an authority on horse and pony breeds worldwide and wrote more than 30 books. His love of all things equestrian coloured his writing, clearly evident in the pages of this sumptuous book which he completed shortly before he died – a fitting epitaph to a life lived with horses.*

JOHN PAWSEY

CHELTENHAM GOLD CUP, 2008 Sam Thomas on Denman is led into the winners' enclosure.

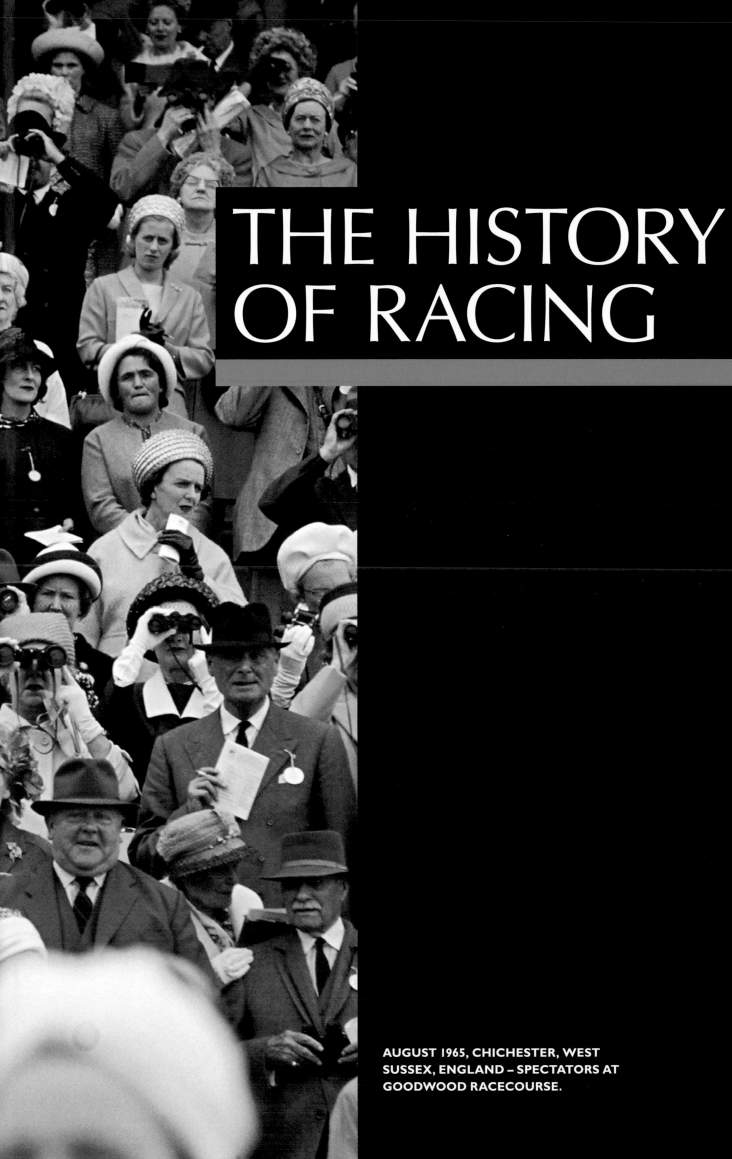

THE HISTORY OF RACING

AUGUST 1965, CHICHESTER, WEST
SUSSEX, ENGLAND – SPECTATORS AT
GOODWOOD RACECOURSE.

The 'Sport of Kings' originates with Britain's Stuart monarchy and the evolution of the world's super-horse, the Thoroughbred, in the 17th–18th centuries.

Harness racing, based largely on the Standardbred, is enormously popular in Europe and America, but there are also important Flat meetings for Arabs, Quarter Horses and even Akhal-Tekes.

This book describes the world's leading racecourses and also features the outstanding personalities, equine and human, who have created the vast, multi-billion-dollar global industry of the racehorse.

THE SPORT OF KINGS

2006 DERBY Sir Percy, ridden by Martin Dwyer, comes home to win the greatest flat race in the world, the Derby at Epsom, England. This rollercoaster course, putting a premium on stamina and balance, regularly attracts record crowds.

CHELTENHAM The Cheltenham course at Prestbury Park, Gloucestershire, England, is noted for its long and testing uphill finish. The Cheltenham Festival, staging the famous Gold Cup is, without doubt, the most important jumping meeting in the world, eclipsing even the unique National meeting at Aintree.

RED MILE America is the world's leading harness-racing nation and the prestigious Red Mile Raceway, so named because of its surface of red clay, is one of its oldest tracks. It was founded in 1875 by the Kentucky Trotting Horse Breeders' Association at Lexington, Kentucky.

THE EARLY HISTORY

Organised racing and matches between individuals were integral to the British sporting scene long before the sport became established in mainland Europe. Moreover, it had the advantage from its earliest days of royal patronage. The Romans were staging races around the town of York as early as the third century AD and, indeed, the northern counties of England were to play a prominent role in the development of the sport.

THE FIRST RECORDED race meeting took place in AD 1174 in the Smithfield area just outside London, England.

The first of the royal patrons of the sport was Henry VIII (1491–1547) who, for all his succession of wives, was a man of considerable accomplishment, a scholar of note and a gifted musician. He was also a devotee of the chase and of the sport of racing, maintaining large studs at the Royal Paddocks at Hampton and importing Spanish and Italian horses that may well have been influenced by Eastern blood.

Other royal studs housed the native 'running' stock, which would have been crossed with the imported horses, those selected for racing being trained at Greenwich under the Master of the Horse.

Henry's daughter, Elizabeth I (1533–1603), continued with the breeding policies instituted by her father and founded another stud at Tutbury in Staffordshire. But it was her successor James I (1566–1625) who first made the town of Newmarket central to the developing sport and ultimately the 'headquarters' of British racing. Himself a skilful horseman, he hunted there, built himself a 'palace' and stabled his hunters and racing stock in the town. Records show him to have attended a race on the Heath at Newmarket in March 1619.

His son, the ill-fated Charles I (1600–1649), continued the association, expanding the royal interest and maintaining large studs. From 1625 regular spring and autumn meetings were being held on the Heath and racing was pursued enthusiastically up to the act of regicide in 1649 that deprived Charles of his head and England of her monarchy.

ANCIENT SPORT Chariot racing was a national sport arousing fierce passions in the amphitheatres of Rome, where the specialist quadrigas (four-horse chariots) competed aggressively over a course of seven laps driven by charioteers wearing protective clothing and racing colours.

THE KING'S PLATE (above) Preparations for the running of the King's Plate on Newmarket's Round Course in 1725 (Peter Tillemans, 1684–1734). Regular spring and autumn meetings were held on the Heath from 1625.

ROWLEY MILE (below) Detroit City (right) on the way to winning the Cesarewitch Handicap at Newmarket in October 2006. The famous handicap is the longest race staged over the Rowley Mile course.

CROMWELL'S PURITANICAL Commonwealth saw the royal studs dispersed, while racing, dancing and, for a time, even the Christmas festivals were regarded as sinful and therefore unacceptable.

WITH THE RESTORATION of the Stuart monarchy and the accession of Charles II (1630–85) in 1660, the gentlemen of England embraced the sport of racing with renewed vigour. Charles II continued the development of Newmarket, becoming involved in the formulation of races and the rules under which they were held. The Rowley Mile Course was named after his stallion Old Rowley, which was also a nickname given to the King in recognition of his amorous adventures. In between he instituted in 1665 the famous Newmarket Town Plate, which he won on two occasions. It is still run as a race, open to amateurs, over 4 miles (6.4km) at Newmarket in August.

Racing became increasingly regulated through Charles's reign but the Jockey Club, racing's ruling body, did not, in fact, officially come into existence until 1752 when land was purchased at Newmarket.

Meanwhile, however, the evolution of the English Thoroughbred, the world's fastest purpose-bred horse, and the foundation for today's global industry, was rapidly gaining momentum.

THE ENGLISH THOROUGHBRED, acknowledged as the fastest, most valuable and influential horse in the world, and of near-perfect proportions, evolved in the 17th–18th centuries as a natural corollary to the passionate enthusiasm of the English gentry for racing and its equally strong addiction to gambling.

THE BREED'S EVOLUTION is popularly and loosely attributed to three imported Oriental horses that founded the four principal bloodlines to which all Thoroughbreds can be traced.

In reality, the situation is far more complex and, indeed, the word Thoroughbred does not appear until 1821 in Vol II of the *General Stud Book*, first published by the Jockey Club's agents, Messrs Weatherby, in 1808. In fact, no official definition of the breed was attempted right up to 1970.

The simplistic view is not unacceptable in broad terms but it takes no account of the existence in England of a long-established base stock of 'running horses' bred at the royal studs, nor of numerous Oriental, Spanish and Italian imports made as early as the Roman occupation of Britain when the Romans introduced Eastern blood to native stock.

THE *TURF REGISTER*, compiled by William Pick in the mid-18th century, suggests the presence of some 160 stallions in that period. Half appear to have been what we would now term Arabian, the remainder being Barbs and Turks. The Barb is a North African horse and, though not so widely recognised as the Arabian, was an important influence on the Spanish Horse, considered the first horse of Europe well into the 18th century. The Turks,

possibly lacking the purity of the Arab, inclined towards the Munagli racing strain as did the horses of northern Iran.

These imports were crossed with the native 'running' stock, which was influenced principally by the swift Galloways of the north, the traditional mount of the Border raiders, from which the Fell pony is a descendant, and the Irish Hobby, forerunner of today's Connemara, and replete with Eastern blood introduced by the Celts and reinforced with a later Spanish element. The Galloway, too, benefited from an Eastern influence. Together they formed a natural seed-bed for out-crossing to the imported stock.

It is against this background that the Thoroughbred evolved. However, it would be fallacious to think that the shrewd breeders of the period used the Eastern imports in the interests of greater speed. Indeed, in comparison with the 'plaine bredde' English horses, their speed was negligible. The creators of the Thoroughbred used Eastern horses because the purity of their lines ensured a prepotency that enabled them to breed consistently true to type.

THE FIRST OF THE THREE 'Founding Fathers' was the Byerley Turk captured by Captain Robert Byerley at the battle of Buda in the last campaign against the Turkish invaders of Hungary. In July 1690, Byerley, then commanding the 6th Dragoon Guards, rode him at the Battle of

BYERLEY TURK The Byerley Turk was the first of the three founding Oriental sires of the English Thoroughbred and is responsible for the breed's first major bloodline, that of the influential Herod.

the Boyne in Ireland. The Byerley Turk then returned to England to stand at stud at Middridge Hall, County Durham, and then at Goldsborough Hall near York.

The Byerley founded the first of the principal bloodlines, that of Herod (1758), through his son Jigg and his great-grandson Tartar. From the Herod line came horses like Tourbillon and the Tetrarch. Indeed, Herod's progeny won over 1,000 races and established him as one of the most important sires in Thoroughbred history.

THE DARLEY ARABIAN was the most striking of the founding trio and carried the most detailed pedigree. Acquired at Aleppo, Syria, by the British Consul, Thomas Darley, in 1704 he was sent to the Darley home, Aldby Park, in East Yorkshire as a four-year-old. A wonderfully proportioned horse he stood at 15hh (1.5m), larger than most of the early Thoroughbreds. Mated with Betty Leedes, a mare from a documented Oriental line, he produced

the first great racehorse, Flying Childers. His full brother, Bartlett's Childers, sired Squirt, sire of the unregarded Marske who sired the unbeaten Eclipse (see pp.18–19), founder of the second Thoroughbred bloodline, from whom the most influential lines of the 20th and 21st centuries descend, for example Blandford, Phalaris, Son-in-Law, Gainsborough, Boss, Teddy and St Simon. The Darley also heads the direct sire lines of Sun Chariot and Big Game.

THE BACKGROUND of the third foundation stallion, the Godolphin Arabian, is less precisely documented but by far the most romantic. This remarkable horse was probably of the Jilfan strain of the Yemen. Born in 1724, from there he went to Tunis via Syria and with three other horses was presented to the French King by the Bey of Tunis. The popular version of the tale is that he pulled a Parisian water-cart until bought in 1729 by Edward Coke of Derbyshire. After Coke's death in 1733 the horse passed to

Lord Godolphin who sent him to his Gog Magog Stud, Cambridge, to be used as a teaser. Reputedly, he fought the stallion, Hobgoblin, for the favours of the mare Roxana, with whom he sired Lath and Cade. Cade sired Matchem, foaled in 1748, who heads the third of the foundation lines, which led to Hurry On and Precipitation.

THE FOURTH of the tail-male lines is that of Highflyer, the son of Herod, who, with his sire, was the greatest influence in the emergence of the middle-distance Classic Thoroughbred. Highflyer was sold to Richard Tattersall in 1779. When Highflyer died in 1793, he had made a fortune for his owner in stud fees.

RECOGNISED AS the foundation mare of the English Thoroughbred breed is Old Bald Peg, by the Unknown Arabian. Repeat crosses of this mare appear 367,162 times in Big Game's pedigree, 233,579 in Sun Chariot's pedigree and 138,827 in Hyperion's pedigree.

DARLEY ARABIAN (top left) The most attractive of the three founding stallions was, undoubtedly, the Darley Arabian and he was also the most fully documented of the three. This most proportionate horse, standing at 15hh (1.52m), was acquired by Thomas Darley at Aleppo, Syria, in 1704. Through Marske he founded the second Thoroughbred bloodline of Eclipse.

GODOLPHIN ARABIAN (top right) The story of the Godolphin Arabian, the third of the 'founding fathers', is even more remarkable than those of the others. Coming from the noted Jilfan strain, he was born in 1724 and eventually passed into the hands of Lord Godolphin who used him at his Cambridgeshire stud. The Godolphin, through his son Cade, founded the Matchem bloodline of the Thoroughbred.

A HANDFUL OF EXCEPTIONAL horses emerge in the formative years of the Thoroughbred as landmarks in the progression of the racehorse that confirm the overriding influence of the Oriental horse. While the early documentation may be incomplete there can be no doubt that Flying Childers occupies pole position as the first truly great racehorse.

Bred in 1715 by Leonard Childers of Doncaster and sold to the Duke of Devonshire, he was by the Darley Arabian out of Betty Leedes, a mare of exclusive Eastern breeding. He was described as 'the fleetest horse that ever ran at Newmarket or, as generally believed, was ever bred in the world'. Few of his performances were recorded but he achieved some phenomenal times, completing four miles (6.4km) at Newmarket in 6 minutes 40 seconds.

His opponents rarely came within a 'distance' of him, i.e. 240 yards (220m), and he beat Fox, an exceptional horse, by two furlongs (402m) when carrying 9st

(57kg). He retired to stud unbeaten and died at Chatsworth in 1741.

GIMCRACK, 'the sweetest little horse that ever was', was a grandson of the Godolphin Arabian, and stood just over 14hh (1.4m). Bred in 1760, he continues to have his place in turf history after nearly 250 years.

An amazingly tough horse, built to gallop, he had numerous owners including William Wildman, the owner of Eclipse. When in French ownership in 1766 he won a 22½-mile (36km) match completed in under an hour.

Gimcrack won 27 races, his prowess being commemorated in York's Gimcrack Stakes and in the annual Gimcrack dinner where his memory is toasted and winners of the race are guests of honour.

There is also a Gimcrack Club in New York, in the US, in acknowledgement of his impact on the American turf through his son Medley (1766) who was exported

to Virginia. He produced a line of broodmares that crossed with spectacular results with the remarkable Diomed to leave a lasting influence on American breeding.

DIOMED ACHIEVED NOTABILITY as the winner in 1780 of the first Derby when in the ownership of Sir Charles Bunbury, the first 'Dictator of the Turf'. Foaled in 1777, he was by Florizel by Herod with a tail-male line to the Byerley Turk. He was not in the same class as Flying Childers or Gimcrack, but won 11 races, including the Derby, but then seems to have lost interest in racing. The horse was retired to stud but did not live up to expectations. By 1798, when the horse was 21 years old, his stud fee had dropped to a derisory two guineas.

For reasons that are unclear Diomed was sold to John Hoomes in Virginia for 50 guineas and rapidly belied his reputation while increasing his value as a sire. He became rapidly established as a top-class stallion and threw many of the greatest horses in American racing history. The best of his progeny was Sir Archy who had a huge effect on the American Thoroughbred, siring the line that led to Timolean, Boston and the great Lexington.

Diomed died at the age of 31 in 1808.

ELIS, BRED AND OWNED by Lord George Bentinck, the second 'Dictator of the Turf', was not a great horse but he won 11 races including the 1836 St Leger, and is best remembered for the circumstances of that victory. Bentinck had betted heavily on Elis winning the race, but the weekend before the Doncaster meeting he was still stabled at Goodwood and it was assumed he

would not compete, since to walk (which was the customary practice) to Doncaster would take a fortnight. However, Bentinck had secretly commissioned a van, the first horse-box, from a London coachbuilder. Drawn by teams of post horses it delivered Elis, fresh and well, on the day before the race and Elis duly won to the discomfiture of Bentinck's rivals and the financial advantage of his owner. A wheel from Bentinck's van is kept in the Jockey Club premises at Newmarket and the conveyance is further commemorated in Abraham Cooper's portrait of Elis.

CONVERSELY, the French horse Gladiateur and the Hungarian mare Kincsem were great horses, shattering the myth of English Thoroughbred supremacy. Gladiateur, 'The Avenger of Waterloo', was bred by Count Frederic de Lagrange in Normandy. By Monarque, he won the English Triple Crown (the 2,000 Guineas, Derby and St Leger) in 1865, humbling his English rivals. At three and four he dominated European racing, winning the Grand Prix de Paris on his triumphal return from England and his Triple Crown victory and numerous prestigious races thereafter in England and France, among them his 40-length win in the Gold Cup. Following the Franco-Prussian War, Gladiateur was sent to England and sold to the Middle Park Stud. He was put down at Dunmow, Essex in 1876 incapacitated by his chronically diseased feet. Something of a freak horse, he was not successful at stud, but his racing record is unequalled. He is honoured in the French Horse Racing Hall of Fame, by the statue erected in his memory at Longchamp and by the Prix Gladiateur run at that prestigious course.

KINCSEM (1874–87), an icon in her own country, was one of the greatest horses in the history of the sport. She was sired by Cambuscan, a horse owned by Queen Victoria and sold to Ernst von Blaskovitch to stand at the Hungarian National Stud. In her first season in 1876 she was unbeaten in her ten races, as she was in all her 54 races at venues throughout Europe. She came to England in 1878 to win the Goodwood Cup with contemptuous ease, having won the most prestigious races in Europe. Still in von Blaskovitch's ownership her last win, for the third time, was the Hungarian Autumn Oaks in 1879.

She is honoured in the Kincsem Horse Park, Budapest, where her statue stands, at Kincsem Museum Budapest and at Kincsem Farm, Archer, Florida.

Kincsem's progeny included the winners of many important races in central Europe.

FLYING CHILDERS (left) Recognised as the first great racehorse, Flying Childers was acknowledged as being infinitely superior to his contemporaries. Bred in 1715 by Leonard Childers of Doncaster and sold to the Duke of Devonshire, his performances against the clock were legendary. He was by the Darley Arabian out of Betty Leeds.

ELIS (above) Elis was foaled in 1833, by Langar (maternal grandsire of two Derby winners: Attila and Orlando) out of Olympia. He was a good, middle-of-the-road performer and a winner of the 1836 Doncaster St Leger, but is best remembered as the horse who, with his companion Drummer, travelled 'from Goodwood to Doncaster in a plain van'.

ECLIPSE *To the world's end*

On April 1, 1764, the year of the great eclipse, a foal was born at the Cranbourne Lodge Stud of HRH The Duke of Cumberland. He was by Marske out of Spiletta by the unbeaten Regulus and, naturally enough, was named Eclipse. In his two seasons on the turf he was unbeaten, distancing his rivals decisively. He is acclaimed as the prime ancestor of the Thoroughbred and is to be found in the pedigrees of nearly every racehorse in the world. Some 75 per cent of all Derby winners from 1780 have been of the Eclipse line.

On the Duke's death Eclipse was bought by an astute Smithfield meat salesman, William Wildman, finally passing into the hands of Col. Dennis O'Kelly, an Irish adventurer living on his wits and the proceeds of some remarkable wagers.

Eclipse ran his first race at Epsom on May 3, 1769, over 4 miles (6.4km) and run in two heats. Previously he had run in a trial that has become part of the Eclipse legend. An old woman questioned on the trial by the touts replied by saying she had seen a white-legged horse 'running at a monstrous rate' with another horse far behind him. She said that it would never catch him if he ran to the end of the world.

After Eclipse ran away with the first heat O'Kelly laid bets that he would place all five horses by name in the second heat. When challenged, he made the famous reply: 'Eclipse first, and the rest nowhere!'

Eclipse, a chestnut horse with a prominent white leg, was big for his day, standing 15.3hh (1.6m). He was higher at the croup than the wither, but was thick-winded and said to roar in his gallop. He was also of uncertain temper. But he was extraordinarily tough and sound and well able to carry as much as 12st (76kg) over 4 miles run in two heats.

When no opponent could be found to take him on, Eclipse retired to stud at Clay Hall, Epsom, where he sired the winners of 344 races. He died in 1789, two years after O'Kelly, his passing being marked by a prolonged Irish wake.

THE FAMED EQUESTRIAN ARTIST GEORGE STUBBS (1724–1806), WHO PAINTED ECLIPSE AS A SIX-YEAR-OLD, DOES NOT SHOW THE UNUSUAL CONFORMATION ON WHICH MANY CONTEMPORARIES REMARKED: HIS QUARTERS WERE PERCEPTIBLY HIGHER THAN HIS WITHERS.

NEWMARKET – RACING'S HQ

It is 'Royal' Newmarket because of its association with the Stuart monarchy; however, it is better known as the 'headquarters' of racing and is a small English town that revolves around the Thoroughbred racehorse.

HYPERION The statue of Hyperion, Lord Derby's wonder horse and winner of the 1933 Derby and St Leger, stands in pride of place before the Jockey Club Rooms and the unique National Horseracing Museum.

THE 2,800 ACRES (1,130ha) of the famed Heath at Newmarket is the property of the Jockey Club, and includes the Rowley Mile and the July Course – not the oldest courses in the world but probably as famous as any other. There are 40 miles (64km) of turfed training gallops round the town and upwards of 17 miles (27km) of artificially surfaced ones for the 2,500 or so horses trained in 50 yards in and around the town. The boundary on the Racecourse Side, approached from Cambridge, is marked by the National Stud and dominated by the sculpture of a great, rearing horse at the road junctions.

Racing takes place in the spring and autumn on the Rowley Mile Course. The two principal races over the Rowley Mile, both run at the first May meeting, are the 2,000 Guineas and the 1,000 Guineas, two of the five English Classic races (see pp.26–27). The July Course is used in June, July and August and stages the July Cup, widely regarded as the most prestigious of all Europe's major sprints.

In the High Street, the statue of Hyperion, Lord Derby's diminutive wonder horse (he stood just 15hh/1.5m) who won the Derby and St Leger in 1933, stands in pride of place before the imposing Jockey Club Rooms, the building itself flanked by the National Horseracing Museum. The museum encapsulates the history of the sport and its famous participants, such as the legendary Eclipse (see pp.18–19), whose gold-mounted hoof has its place in the Jockey Club Rooms. The museum also displays fascinating memorabilia of the great Fred Archer (see p.90), who committed suicide at his home, Falmouth House, on 8 November 1886, and is reputed to still haunt the scene of his triumphs. He is buried in Newmarket's Dullingham Road Cemetery.

TO EMPHASISE THE ASSOCIATION with the horse as the *raison d'etre* of the town's existence, strings of horses are ridden along the Bury Road and through the town on their way to and from exercise, while traffic pauses, acknowledging their right of way. Just off the High Street, high above the road, are Tattersalls Park Paddocks (see pp.24–25). The Sales Paddocks are pre-eminent in the world of racing and some of the world's most famous horses have been auctioned here.

A hundred years ago Tattersalls sold horses in the street outside the Jockey Club; today a fixed programme of sales is staged through the year, including the July Sale, the flagship October Yearling Sales, and the December Sale. The October Part One is undoubtedly the most important, attracting the attention of the crowds and the big buyers like Sheikh Mohammed of Dubai. He owns the Dalham Hall Stud just outside the town, which is, of course, surrounded on every side by studs breeding the world's super-horse, the English Thoroughbred, that is to all intents synonymous with Newmarket.

NATIONAL HORSERACING MUSEUM (left)
The National Horseracing Museum encapsulates the history of the sport in displays, artefacts and memorabilia. The museum has a collection relating to Fred Archer, the tragic champion who committed suicide in 1886. Nearby, the immortal Eclipse's gold-mounted hoof is displayed in the adjacent Jockey Club Rooms.

NEWMARKET STREETS (below) As befits the headquarters of racing and Thoroughbred breeding, the horse takes precedence in the streets of Newmarket. Traffic pauses to acknowledge the right of way of strings making their way to and from exercise on the gallops and training areas surrounding the Suffolk town and the 2,800 acres (1,130ha) of Newmarket Heath, owned by the Jockey Club and including the racecourses.

ADMINISTRATION

The Jockey Club was racing's governing body for over 200 years. Its roots lie in the mid-18th century when corruption was rife in the sport and rules virtually non-existent. However, at its inception it was in no way intended to become a regulatory body. It was formed by a group of aristocrats and gentlemen owners to meet together, arrange matches between their horses and settle bets.

IN THOSE EARLY DAYS the Jockey Club met at inns in Pall Mall, St James's Street and Bond Street in London, moving to Newmarket in 1752 and erecting a Coffee Room at the site of the present Jockey Club building. It rapidly began to influence the sport: formulating rules, settling disputes, creating disciplinary procedures and then licensing participants. In the following century it produced three great reformers, often termed 'Dictators of the Turf'. The first was Sir Charles Bunbury, who won the first Derby (1780) with Diomed after, it is said, tossing a coin with Lord Derby for the privilege of naming the race. He was followed by Lord George Bentinck (1802–48), a man wielding great influence through force of character. The third and most famous 'Dictator' was Admiral John Henry Rous (1795–1887). These three laid the foundations for today's global industry and were a powerful influence in the development of the modern Thoroughbred.

FOR ALMOST all of its history the Jockey Club was a self-elected, autocratic body. However, it has always commanded great respect and served racing well.

Of necessity, a controlling body has to be supported by meticulously kept records, which, of course, are also vital in the development of any breed. From 1770, when James Weatherby was appointed Keeper of the *Match Book*, the Weatherby family was the highly efficient secretariat for the Club – its own civil service, in fact. The firm maintains the *General Stud Book*, which it founded, producing the first volume in 1791. It also publishes the *Racing Calendar* and continues to service much of the business of racing.

INEVITABLY, an elite autocracy would become unacceptable in an increasingly democratic society, and in 1993, the Jockey Club skilfully began to concede its power base by the formation of the British Horseracing Board, which developed into the present governing and regulatory body for the sport, the British Horseracing Authority, with powers extending over every aspect of racing. It also represents British racing abroad and is a founder member of the International Federation of Horseracing Authorities.

Nonetheless, the Jockey Club remains at the heart of British racing and is now able to concentrate upon its commercial activities, the ownership of racecourses, the Jockey Club estates, like those at Newmarket and Lambourn, the National Stud and the extensive Newmarket properties.

GETTING RESULTS The end product of an effective administrative operation: These two Thoroughbreds fighting out a finish epitomise the spirit of the sport of Flat racing.

TATTERSALLS

Tattersalls, auctioneers of Thoroughbred horses, is a
racing institution and integral to the industry.

THE FIRM WAS FOUNDED by Richard Tattersall who left Yorkshire, in northern England, in 1745 to purchase an interest in Beevor's Horse Repository in London and become manager of the Duke of Kingston's stud. Later he leased land and premises at Hyde Park Corner where he staged twice-weekly sales and where, for a while, the fledgling Jockey Club had a subscription room for betting between its members. In 1815 larger Rooms were opened there for a new breed of gamblers and bookmakers. By 1856 the club, known as the Ring, had 400 members paying two guineas a year and settling their debts each Monday morning. The club is remembered in

Tattersalls' Ring, 'Tatts', the betting ring that is to be found on every racecourse.

Tattersall himself, a shrewd businessman and a good judge of horses, was the first commercial breeder of the Thoroughbred. It was he who in 1799 acquired Highflyer, the son of Herod, founder of one of the tail-male lines of the breed.

Richard's son, Edmund, moved the business to Knightsbridge Green in 1865 selling a variety of stock, racehorses, hunters and even hounds, up to the Second World War when operations were transferred entirely to Newmarket, where Tattersalls had conducted regular Thoroughbred auctions since the end of the 18th century. These sales were later

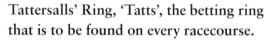

OUTSIDE PARADE (left) The Sales Paddocks at Newmarket with *The Fox* cupola, topped with a bust of George IV, at its centre. The Paddock and Sales Ring were designed by Sir Albert Richardson, who also designed the Jockey Club building in the High Street.

moved to land purchased behind Queensbury House in 1884, the site of the present Park Paddocks. Thereafter, Tattersalls was to become recognised as the premier bloodstock auctioneers in the world. Peter Willett, accepted authority on the Thoroughbred horse, wrote that: 'Between 1949 and 1984, 38 winners of 41 British classic races were sold by Tattersalls as either foals or yearlings...'

FORMALLY OPENED IN 1965, the Paddock and the magnificent Sale Ring were designed by Sir Albert Richardson, President of the Royal Academy, who had also designed the 1934 Jockey Club building in the High Street. It was he who insisted upon and arranged the erection of *The Fox* which had stood at Tattersalls since the 1780s and also of the famous arch, which had also stood at Hyde Park Corner. *The Fox*, a remarkable piece of statuary, symbolises the origins of Tattersalls, when the trade was largely with hunters.

It is a cupola topped with a bust of George IV, a good customer of the firm, in which sits a cleverly modelled fox on a rather grand plinth. To get *The Fox* to Newmarket the cupola had to be cut in sections and re-assembled on its new site.

Tattersalls hold regular sales at Newmarket: the July, the October, the Autumn and December, of which the October Part One is the most important by some way.

Two years after the official opening, at the 1967 December Sales, the two-year-old Vaguely Noble entered the ring and in two minutes 12 seconds was sold for the then world record price of £136,000. Vaguely Noble won the 1968 Prix de l'Arc de Triomphe and became a leading stallion in Kentucky.

Ten years later the Houghton (now the October Part One) aggregate price was seven million guineas; in 1983 three horses were sold for over a million guineas each and Sheikh Mohammed set a European sales record in 1998 when he bought a yearling for three million guineas.

TATTERSALLS SALES Tattersalls' Sale Ring at Park Paddocks, Newmarket, is world renowned, and some of the most expensive horses in the world have changed hands there. The two-year-old Vaguely Noble, winner of the 1968 l'Arc de Triomphe and afterwards a leading stalllion in Kentucky, US, was sold there in 1967.

THE CLASSICS

The English 'Classics', introduced in the late 18th century, mark the watershed in the development of the modern Thoroughbred and the movement towards the production of early maturing stock giving owners a quicker return on their financial outlay. This, indeed, was the period during which racing was becoming regularised and a recognisable season becoming evident. The institution of the Classics was, in essence, therefore, a recognition of that fact.

SUFFRAGETTES AT THE DERBY Tragedy struck the Epsom Derby of 1913 when Emily Davison, a leading member of the Suffragette movement, threw herself at King George V's horse Anmer. The horse, galloping at full speed, was brought down and Emily Davison lost her life.

PREVIOUSLY, THE EMPHASIS in breeding was on stamina with horses not starting their career until five or six years of age, like today's chasers. Horses like Eclipse raced over distances of up to four miles and might run two heats in one day, which speaks volumes for the soundness and stamina of the early Thoroughbred. The Classics are for three-year-olds and put the accent on young horses, carrying light weights and running over far shorter distances at far greater speeds. The concept was vigorously encouraged by Sir Charles Bunbury who held that the future of the breed depended on the development of speed. HH The Aga Khan, the most powerful force in racing in the 1930s, summed it up as 'speed, more speed and yet more speed'.

The English Classics are comprised of five races for three-year-olds. The oldest, first run in 1776, is the St Leger, named after Col. Anthony St Leger of Park Hill, a prominent member of the Jockey Club. Held at Doncaster, where race meetings

ST LEGER WINNER The Maharajah of Baroda leading in Sayajirao, winner of the 1947 St Leger at Doncaster. The race, for colts and fillies, was first run in 1776. It is named after Col. Anthony St Leger and is the oldest of the English Classics.

have been held since 1595, it is for colts and fillies and is run in September over 1¾ miles (2.8km). The 2,000 Guineas and the 1,000 Guineas (for fillies) were first held in 1809 and 1814 respectively and are run at Newmarket in May over 1 mile (1.6km). The Oaks (for fillies) was first run in 1779 and named after the Earl of Derby's house, the Oaks at Epsom. It is run over 1½ miles (2.4km) in early June; the first Oaks was won, appropriately enough, by Lord Derby's Bridget. The male counterpart of the Oaks, the Derby, was first run on Epsom Downs in 1780.

The Triple Crown, racing's greatest accolade, is won by those horses winning the 2,000 Guineas (or 1,000 Guineas), the Derby (or Oaks) and the St Leger.

THE ENGLISH CLASSICS act as a pattern for similar events held by the world's racing nations. The American equivalents are the Kentucky Derby, the Preakness Stakes, the Belmont Stakes and the Coaching Club American Oaks, the first three constituting the American Triple Crown. The Kentucky Derby, ¼ mile (0.4km) shorter than the Epsom prototype, is held in May at Churchill Downs, Kentucky, over 10 furlongs (2km).

The Preakness, over 9½ furlongs (1.9km) is run at Pimlico, Baltimore, a fortnight after the Derby, and the Belmont Stakes, over 12 furlongs (2.4km), at Belmont Park, Long Island, within three weeks after that. (Belmont Park is close to where Richard Nicolls, first governor of New York, with an admirable sense of priorities, laid out the first American racecourse in 1664.)

PERSIMMON Epsom's greeting to Persimmon, being led in by HRH Prince (Albert) Edward after winning the Derby of 1896, was tumultuous and sustained. Persimmon was trained by Richard Marsh and ridden by John Watts. The future king won the race again in 1900 with Diamond Jubilee.

GAMBLING – THE FOUNDATION

The development of racing is bound inextricably with the practice of betting, which might be considered almost a sport in its own right and one followed by punters all over the world, whatever national laws may pertain. Richard Tattersall, the bloodstock auctioneer, asked by a Special Committee on the Gaming Laws set up in 1844 whether the abolition of betting would affect horse breeding, replied, unequivocally, 'If betting were put an end to there would be an end to my breeding'.

SUCCESSIVE BRITISH GOVERNMENTS have sought to balance betting as an important source of revenue against what was felt to be a morally dubious issue that had to be contained by gaming laws for the general good.

Sporting men of the 18th century laid wagers one against the other and/or as members of private clubs, which were unaffected by the law, such as that meeting at the Tattersall's Subscription Rooms at Hyde Park Corner. They were, indeed, compulsive gamblers, prepared to win and lose fortunes, which many did. For them gambling was as much a passion as the actual matching of their horses. It would have been unthinkable to have had it any other way.

THE LAWS ON GAMBLING differ widely from one racing nation to another. In 1908, for example, the state of New York banned racing itself – the Charles Evans Hughes ban, countered by the English Jersey Act of 1913 – which could have had a disastrous effect on American Thoroughbred breeding. The Act was not, indeed, modified until 1949, but today there still remain ambiguities in the betting laws of individual states.

HAVING A FLUTTER There is no shortage of punters eager to lay money on their fancied horses. For most race-goers betting is integral to attendance at the race meeting. In Britain, as late as 1961, off-course betting was prohibited by law, but that is far from being the case today, when betting in a variety of ways, including on-line, is commonplace.

In Britain, until as late as 1961, off-course betting was prohibited by law. To place a bet in those circumstances it was necessary to have a credit account with a bookmaker or one was compelled to use a bookie's runner and risk prosecution in consequence. Not before time, the law was changed. Today, there are licensed betting shops in every small town, on-line betting is commonplace, and the big companies, in their own interest, are major sponsors of the sport. In fact, betting is recognised as an integral part of the industry, or, indeed, an industry in its own right, with much coverage being given to it while TV programmes are centred on the betting gurus. Swiftly following legalisation, came the Horseracing Betting Levy Board, responsible for the levy from betting proceeds, which was to be used for 'the improvement of breeds of horse, the advancement or encouragement of veterinary science or veterinary education and the improvement of horseracing' – laudable aims, indeed, since off-course betting reduced attendances at racecourses.

Bets can be placed by means of a deposit account with a bookmaker. Or, for the perversely minded, you can 'lay' horses, i.e. bet to lose, with the betting exchanges.

Punters can bet to win or go 'each way', i.e. win and place. They can bet on a 'double' (two selections in two events), or a 'treble', or an 'accumulator' as well as a number of more arcane permutations.

Then there is the Tote (the *Pari-Mutuel* in France), where returns are sometimes lower but invariably will be much higher when backing long-priced horses, sometimes as much as 100–1 for horses with a starting price of about 33–1.

FLAT RACING

Although courses round the world conform in their essentials, there are notable differences between the traditional courses in Britain and Ireland and those further afield. All-weather tracks are now increasingly evident and some venues are entirely dependent upon them. In America and elsewhere, horses are stabled and trained on the course rather than in private yards, which are the norm in Britain and Ireland. In common to all courses, however, is the on-going process of improvement to attract the audiences vital to the viability of the sport.

COURSES OF THE WORLD

DUBAI (above) An ancient sport against a modern background: A horse trains on the Godolphin track in front of the fast-growing international centre of Dubai. Although Flat racing's roots lie in the West, the injection of Middle Eastern wealth is an important influence on the sport today.

PIMLICO, US (left) The dirt track at Pimlico racecourse, Maryland, is typical of American courses, creating 'kickback' in the faces of horses and riders. Most European courses traditionally race on turf.

COURSES IN EUROPE

It is no surprise that the UK, with its history of royal racing patronage, is home to some of the oldest and most famous courses in Europe, and indeed, the world. At the very epicentre of thoroughbred racing is Newmarket.

NEWMARKET is situated some 70 miles (113km) northeast of London, partly in Suffolk and partly in Cambridgeshire. It was Charles II who made the town and the course a centre for racing (see pp.20–21) and the Rowley Mile is named after 'Old Rowley', the nickname of the King's favourite hack. Major races run over the Rowley Mile track include the first two British Classics (see pp.26–27): the 2,000 Guineas, generally contested by just colts, and the 1,000 Guineas for fillies. At the other end of the season, Newmarket stages 'Champions Day', a one-afternoon extravaganza headlined by the extremely valuable Champion Stakes, a 1¼ miles (2km) Group 1 contest won in imperious fashion in 2008 by the same year's Derby winner New Approach, whose Newmarket performance earned him the honour of being crowned the best horse in the world in 2008. Also staged on Champions Day is the Cesarewitch, a marathon handicap that forms the second half of the 'autumn double', a two-race punting puzzle that begins with the Cambridgeshire, a September cavalry charge contested by a huge field over a straight 1¹/₈ miles (1.8km). Within binocular view of the Rowley Mile is the July Course, Newmarket's popular summer track famed for its Friday night

NEWMARKET Frankie Dettori executes his famous flying dismount from the American-bred filly Sander Camillo after winning the 2006 Chippenham Lodge Stud Cherry Hinton Stakes on Newmarket's popular July Course.

meetings and the three-day July Festival, a fixture highlighted by Europe's most prestigious sprint, the six-furlong (1.2km) July Cup.

EPSOM, however, is probably the most famous of the British courses as the home of the greatest Flat race in the world, the Derby. With a premium on handling the contours, Epsom is probably the most demanding track of any in the world. The Derby course climbs uphill for over 100ft (30m) before dropping sharply to Tattenham Corner and rising again in the last furlong. Only a supremely balanced horse of good conformation can cope with the bends, gradients and camber that throws unbalanced horses towards the far rail of the home straight. One day before the Derby are the equivalent race for fillies, the Oaks, and the Coronation Cup, a race designed to attract the previous year's Derby and Oaks winners.

In 2007, crowds of over 100,000 witnessed Frankie Dettori winning the Derby at his fifteenth attempt on the red-hot favourite Authorized. On the previous day, trainer Henry Cecil, recovering from cancer and having produced no Classic winners for seven years, created a record by winning the Oaks for the eighth time with Light Shift.

EPSOM (top right) Epsom is only 15 miles (24km) from the centre of London and draws enthusiastic crowds for the Derby. By the middle of the 19th century even Parliament did not sit on Derby day.

DERBY DAY (right) Epsom has its own unique carnival atmosphere with thousands enjoying the huge fairground and picnicking on the downs.

ASCOT, in Berkshire and 30 miles west of London, was founded in 1711 by Queen Anne and remains the property of the Crown. A right-handed turf track, which has to its inside a jumps course, Ascot stages 25 race days each year of which the most famous and prestigious is Royal Ascot, a five-day fixture that embraces the finest Flat racing, the very best in fashion and the glorious pageantry of a daily royal procession.

An extensive £200 million redevelopment programme involving a new grandstand, extended facilities and major alterations to the racing surface and paddocks was completed in 2006. It was an impressive achievement but not without teething troubles caused largely as a result of the limited visibility afforded from the stand.

Major races held at Ascot include the King George VI and Queen Elizabeth Stakes (1½ miles/2.4km), the most important all-aged Flat race run in Britain and very often the scene of mighty clashes between the Derby winner and the top older horses. The track also hosts the Queen Elizabeth II Stakes, otherwise known as the mile championship of Europe, and the 2½ miles Gold Cup (4km), the more than 200-year-old centrepiece of the Royal meeting and the the blue riband for the Flat's long-distance runners.

The Ascot course, also famous for some of the winter's biggest jumps races, is triangular, and some 14 furlongs (2.8km) long. It runs downhill to Swinley Bottom and then rises for a mile (1.6km) to the finish. Tradition dictates that a bell is rung as runners swing into Ascot's short home straight, the scene of the 1975 King George battle between Grundy and Bustino, regarded by many as the most pulsating finish in racing history.

ROYAL ASCOT HM Queen Elizabeth II takes part in the Royal Procession at the newly redeveloped Royal Ascot in 2006. The June Royal Ascot meeting is the most prestigious event held at the course.

CORRECT ATTIRE A strict dress code is enforced in the Royal Enclosure at Royal Ascot, including top hats for gentlemen and an appropriate hat or substantial fascinator for ladies.

FURTHER SOUTH, 65 miles (105km) from London, on the Sussex downland that is part of the Duke of Richmond's estate, is Goodwood, the most beautiful Flat racecourse in England and worthy of the adjective 'Glorious'.

The course was built by the third Duke in 1801 on an undulating right-hand track, which while not severe provides challenges not found elsewhere and certainly demands particular skills on the part of the jockeys. The sub-soil of chalk ensures excellent drainage and usually good, consistent going but only a well-made, balanced horse will cope with the turns and dips.

The principal five-day summer meeting, which traditionally spans the handover from July to August, is staged under the umbrella title of Glorious Goodwood, and

is very much a cornerstone of England's summer social calendar.

Highlight of the meeting is the Group 1 Sussex Stakes, one of Europe's premier mile features, while the Nassau Stakes (1¼ miles/2km) is a top-flight contest for fillies and mares. The Goodwood Cup, though no longer run over the lung-bursting trip of 2⅝ miles (4.2km) is still, at 2 miles (3.2km), a true test for the very best stayers. For the speedsters, the six-furlong (1.2km) Stewards' Cup is a sprint handicap that figures among the year's most eagerly awaited and hard-to-solve handicaps.

Goodwood stages a number of other quality races, not least the Celebration Mile, a race won in 2008 by Raven's Pass en route to victory in America's world championship Flat race, the Breeders' Cup Classic.

GOODWOOD Racegoers watch the field pass during the Sportsman Newspaper Handicap race on the first day of the July meeting known as Glorious Goodwood. The undulating right-hand track places specific demands on both horses and jockeys.

BROWN JACK *Sterling qualities*

Every so often racing throws up an equine phenomenon who captures the imagination and affection of the public to an extraordinary degree. Inevitably, they are jumpers, geldings whose careers span a number of seasons like Arkle and Desert Orchid. Brown Jack was just such a one and, along with Arkle, perhaps, was the most popular horse to have ever raced in Britain. Such was his impact on people in all walks of life that a clergyman preaching at Wroughton, where the horse was trained, felt able to take as his 'text' Brown Jack's sterling qualities of courage, perseverance and kindliness.

Bred in Ireland in 1924 by the stayer, Jackdaw, sire of two Grand National winners, out of a very tough mare from jumping lines, Querquidella, he was destined to race over fences.

He started racing over hurdles, crowning a successful record with a good victory in the Champion Hurdle at Cheltenham. While clearly a notable performer, it is there that any similarity to the established jumping favourites ends, for, uniquely, it was on the Flat, in partnership with his jockey Steve Donoghue, that he made his reputation as the greatest equine character of his time. It began in 1928 and his first big win was in the prestigious 2½ mile (4km) Ascot Stakes, which he took with contemptuous ease. That was the beginning of his long association with Royal Ascot, where he was to win six consecutive victories in Britain's longest race, the 2¾ mile (4.4km) Queen Alexandra Stakes.

A naturally indolent horse, or just a very intelligent one who played to the crowd outrageously, Brown Jack never exerted himself more than was necessary to win. In addition to their Ascot successes the 'old firm' of Donoghue and Brown Jack won the Goodwood Cup, the Ebor and the Rosebery Memorial Handicap, all on the sort of turning tracks that Brown Jack favoured.

The partnership won its last Queen Alexandra in 1934, when Brown Jack was ten, amid unprecedented scenes that were not to be repeated until Frankie Dettori completed the 'magnificent seven' (winning every race on the card) 62 years later.

In retirement, Brown Jack lived at Sir Harold Wernher's home, Thorpe Lubenham Hall, where he died after contracting a chill in 1948.

CHAMPION RACEHORSE BROWN JACK, RIDDEN HERE BY H. LANG INSTEAD OF HIS MOST FAMOUS JOCKEY, STEVE DONOGHUE, IN 1934.

HORSES HAVE RUN OVER Ireland's Curragh from time immemorial and it is one of the world's greatest courses. It is the Newmarket of Ireland and stages all of that country's five Classic races. The Curragh, near Newbridge, Co. Kildare, is hard by what was the British Army headquarters up to 1922. It is a wide, galloping, right-handed 2-mile (3.2km) horseshoe and is regarded as a severe test of stamina, more so, indeed, than the Epsom course. A new grandstand was built after the Irish Hospitals Sweepstakes encouraged the change from the title Irish Derby to Irish Sweeps Derby in 1962, and at that time surrounding landowners gave up their rights of common grazing on the Curragh, allowing the course to be fenced and a watering system to be installed. The Irish Derby was first run in 1866 and the Irish Oaks a year before that. However, not until 1946 were the five Irish Classics properly established.

The Derby double (a win at both Epsom and the Curragh) has been achieved by horses of the calibre of Shergar, Nijinsky, Grundy, The Minstrel, Shirley Heights and Troy, while the Irish Oaks has always attracted a strong line-up bolstered by top French fillies. Marcel Boussac, for instance, won it in 1950 with Corejada, although the 1973 edition is still regarded as the best ever run. It was won by Dahlia, who in the following week scored a famous victory in the King George VI and the Queen Elizabeth II Stakes at Ascot.

CURRAGH (top) The horseshoe-shaped course at Curragh is a great test of a horse's stamina. For this reason, the Irish Derby is regarded as at least as challenging as Epsom's Derby – if not more so.

PUNCHESTOWN (above) This course is home to the Irish equivalent of the Cheltenham Festival. The five-day Punchestown Festival in late April lets Ireland's top jumpers meet their British counterparts on home turf.

Major races at the Curragh, the five Group 1 Classics apart, include the National Stakes, Ireland's premier race for two-year-olds, the Moyglare Stud Stakes and the Phoenix Stakes.

PUNCHESTOWN, situated 22 miles (35km) from Dublin city centre but just a good walk from the town of Naas, has been the home of national hunt racing in Ireland since 1827. For five days in late April, the track, set amidst 450 acres of stunning countryside, welcomes thousands of visitors for the Irish National Hunt Festival, at which 3 million euro is raced for by Ireland's best jumpers as well as some of Britain's finest chasers and hurdlers.

LEOPARDSTOWN, a very popular track with Irish racegoers, is in the Dublin suburb of Foxrock, about 3 miles (5km) from the city centre. Ireland's leading dual-purpose track, its left-handed circuit is scene of the country's definitive all-aged Flat race, the Irish Champion Stakes, while jumps fans are blessed with a host of goodies, not least the four-day Christmas Festival. Over the following weeks, Leopardstown attracts top-class fields for the ultra-competitive Pierse Handicap Hurdle, the Grade 1 Irish Champion Hurdle and Ireland's most prestigious chase, the Hennessy Gold Cup.

Leopardstown opened in 1888 and was acquired, at the end of the 1960s by the Irish Racing Board, which is responsible for the new stands and excellent facilities.

LEOPARDSTOWN (top) Fantastic Light (right), ridden by Frankie Dettori, battles his way to a narrow victory over Galileo, ridden by Michael Kinane in the 2001 Irish Champion Stakes held at Leopardstown.

LEOPARDSTOWN (above) Studmaster (third from right) on his way to a win at Leopardstown. The grandstands and facilities at this racecourse are frequently upgraded and are renowned for their quality.

IN THE EARLIER YEARS of the 19th century, racing in France suffered from a lack of suitable courses, a situation largely overcome by the foundation of the course at Longchamp, where a meeting was held in 1857, and at Chantilly, the principal training area in France, where racing was established even earlier in 1834.

Longchamp is sited in the Bois de Boulogne on the outskirts of Paris, and stages some 20 Group 1 races including the famous Prix de l'Arc de Triomphe, arguably Europe's single most important Flat race, and the French 1,000 and 2,000 Guineas, both of which are held on a single Sunday in May. The Longchamp track is right-handed and runs round 1 mile 6 furlongs (2.8km), with other distances being accommodated by the use of the various loops incorporated into the course. The track rises in the back straight and falls as it enters the comparatively short home straight. The ground is well watered and firm going occurs only rarely.

Of all Longchamp's many features, it is the Arc that dominates like no other. The 1½ miles (2.4km) prize is by far the most valuable horserace run in Europe, and rightly so, as it brings the very best thoroughbreds from France, Britain, Ireland, and sometimes even America and Japan, for an always spellbinding treat. Its 2008 winner, the Aga Khan's brilliant filly Zarkava, followed in the footsteps of equine champions like Sea-Bird, Dancing Brave, Ribot and Peintre Celebre, all of which claimed Flat racing's most sought-after prize.

CHANTILLY, surrounded by some of the most famous training gallops in the world,

is 27 miles (44km) north of Paris and the home of the Prix du Jockey-Club and the Prix de Diane, the French Derby and Oaks equivalents respectively.

The course, despite its position, has only a few days racing a year. In addition, the track is noted for the complexity of its layout. Essentially, it is right-handed, 1 mile 5 furlongs (2.6km) in circumference with a 3-furlong (0.6km) straight and a 9-furlong (1.8km) straight course. Dominating the view from the Chantilly grandstands is a château that houses a host of sumptuous stables, known as Les Grandes Écuries, which were built by the delightfully barmy seventh Prince de Condé, who believed he was to be reincarnated as a horse.

OTHER DISTINCTIVE FRENCH COURSES are those at Deauville, the fashionable holiday resort in Normandy, where polo, golf and the beaches are additional attractions. Deauville also stages the most important yearling sales in France.

The famous track at Maisons-Laffitte, on the banks of the Seine is, like Chantilly, centred on a large training area, although here it is jumpers that predominate.

A number of those jumpers race at Auteuil, France's top jumps track and home of the famous Grand Steeple-Chase de Paris.

LONGCHAMP (left) The course's most famous race is undoubtedly the Prix de l'Arc de Triomphe, run on the first Sunday in October. This prestigious event has been the scene of memorable triumphs for some of racing's truly great horses.

CHANTILLY (above) Overlooked by the fairytale Château de Chantilly, the course is an attractive venue with excellent grandstands, the whole dominated by the impressive Grandes Écuries, the palatial stables built for the Prince de Condé.

MAISONS-LAFFITTE (top right) Little Tommy Fella, ridden by his owner Gina Rarick, exercises on the famous training fields at Maisons-Laffitte. The Maisons-Laffitte track is at the heart of one of the biggest equestrian training centres in Europe.

THE MOST ATTRACTIVE of the German courses and the Federal Republic's equivalent of Deauville is at Baden-Baden, the spa resort in the foothills of the Black Forest. In fact, the course is at the village of Iffezheim, about 12 miles (19km) from the city, but is easily accessible.

Founded in the mid-19th century by the local casino operator, Baden-Baden owed much of its popularity to the patronage of King Edward VII, who was a frequent visitor. The course is a left-handed one, 10 furlongs (2km) in circumference with a 3-furlong (0.6km) straight, and incorporates a figure-of-eight jumps course. Race meetings are in May, June and through August and September. The major race at Baden-Baden is the 1½ mile (2.4km) Grosser Preis von Baden, which for many years was dominated by foreign horses. Two horses have won the Grosser Preis three times: the Hungarian mare Kincsem in 1877–79 and the German Oleander, who won between 1927 and 1929.

THE FIRST GERMAN DERBY was run in 1869 at the Hamburg Racing Club (Hamburger Reun-Club) course, 3 miles (5km) from the city centre, and was originally known as the Norddeutsches Derby, an event over 2,050 yards (1,875m) for three-year-old colts, fillies and geldings.

Very soon, however, this most English of the German courses changed to the Epsom Derby distance. The race is dominated by locally trained horses, but British trainers and jockeys are usually much in evidence.

Unusually, the right-handed course is completely flat. Its circumference is 10 furlongs (2km) and the straight is 2½ furlongs (0.5km). In the centre of the course is the diagonal steeplechase track.

ALTHOUGH COLOGNE COURSE is arguably less important in the scenario of German racing, the Kölner Rennverein (Cologne Racing Club) hosts the internationally renowned Preis von Europa, a 2,624 yards (2,400m) Group 1 race open to three-year-olds and older horses of all countries.

Like Baden-Baden and Hamburg, Cologne also includes a jumping course.

ITALIAN RACING, like Germany's, is generally one rung below the sport staged in Britain, Ireland and France. However,

the country still has great races and racecourses, not least Capannelle, backed by the majestic Castelli Hills, on the Via Appia Nuova just outside the city. Founded in 1881, it is the home of the Italian Derby and the first two Italian classics, the 2,000 and 1,000 Guineas. Over 50 trainers are centred at Capannelle where the flat, right-handed course is very well drained at all times.

The course at San Siro, Milan, is also a training centre with extensive facilities, including a steeplechase schooling ground. It is considered to be one of Europe's finest courses and is with justification known as 'the course of truth' for its ability to measure the worth and, in particular, the stamina of a racehorse.

SAN SIRO (above) Electrocutionist, the 2005 winner of the Gran Premio Milano, leads the parade at the beautiful San Siro racecourse. The course, with its fine training facilities, is deservedly known as one of Europe's finest.

BADEN-BADEN (left) The field thunders past the stands at the historic Baden-Baden racecourse. The left-handed course is the setting for the renowned Grosser Preis von Baden in early September.

COURSES IN AUSTRALASIA, ASIA AND THE MIDDLE EAST

The global appeal of Thoroughbred racing is reflected in the proliferation of top-class courses throughout the Middle East, Asia and Australasia. In Australia, the foundation for Melbourne's world-famous Flemington course had been laid within five years of the arrival of the first settlers in 1835.

On the Indian subcontinent, racecourses of a kind were to be found at most up-country stations early in the century with organised racing being centred, originally, on the magnificently opulent courses created at the old Presidency cities of Madras, Calcutta and Bombay. The Bombay (now Mumbai) Mahalakshmi course retains, remarkably, its old title: the

FLEMINGTON (above) Situated in Melbourne, Victoria, Flemington racecourse is home to the prestigious Melbourne Cup, Australia's richest horse race, held in November.

MUMBAI (right) Pagentry still holds strong at Mumbai's Mahalakshami course where the runners and riders are led out by a ceremonial rider before Classic races.

MUMBAI (top right) Crowds cheer the winner of the 2007 McDowell Indian Derby, Diabolical, ridden by Colm O'Donoghue. The Derby is one of India's most highly regarded racing events.

Royal Western India Turf Club. It stages its own Classic races within some 30 days racing a year, while also holding auction sales in conjunction with the more important meetings.

Racecourses built in the heyday of the Raj complemented the grandeur of imperial municipal architecture, although they were infinitely more comfortable and intimate. The Mahalakshmi course is no exception but like no other it is remarkable for its situation, being separated from the sea by the width of a dual carriageway

and driving a green wedge into an otherwise unbroken crescent of white concrete pressing on the water's edge.

FURTHER EAST, the influence of empire is evident in the Happy Valley course built on Hong Kong Island in 1845 and rebuilt in 1995, and in the fantastic Sha Tin complex built in 1978 on the Chinese mainland north of the Kowloon Hills. Both are managed by the Hong Kong Jockey Club and are assured of large attendances and incomes by the Chinese passion for gambling.

Happy Valley, right-handed and less than 7 furlongs (1.4km) in circumference, is probably the tightest track in the world and particularly difficult to ride because the turns are not cambered.

CONVERSELY, Sha Tin (the name means Sand Fields) is a highly sophisticated, state-of-the-art racing centre that can hardly be matched anywhere in the world and includes unrivalled facilities for gambling. A right-handed track, it comprises a 2,078-yard (1,900m) grass track and a 1,094-yard (1,000m) straight, an all-weather circuit and a training track for the use of horses stabled in 10 two-storey blocks – all air-conditioned and replete with piped music. The stands, covering over 16 acres (6.4ha), accommodate over 30,000 people and face the world's biggest

SHA TIN (above) The enclosed parade ring and modern grandstands at Sha Tin amply demonstrate the unrivalled state-of-the-art facilities at this Chinese racecourse.

HAPPY VALLEY (left) This aerial view of Happy Valley shows the racecourse nestling among the skyscrapers on Hong Kong Island. The original 1845 course was rebuilt in 1995.

HAPPY VALLEY (right) The right-handed, uncambered course at Happy Valley presents particular challenges to horse and rider. Here, Andreas Starke wins the Cathay Pacific International Jockeys Championships in 2005.

video matrix screen, which allows races to be viewed and re-played in their entirety.

THE OLDEST ESTABLISHED COURSE in Malaysia is at Bukit Timah, 7 miles (11km) from Singapore City. It was founded in 1842 and is probably the biggest betting centre in Asia.

PHAR LAP *Australia's hero*

The name Phar Lap is the Sinhalese for 'Lightning', and the big chestnut gelding (17hh/1.7m) was also admiringly nicknamed 'The Red Terror'. Contemporaries described him as a 'phenomenal racing machine' and by Australians he is still regarded as the greatest racehorse ever foaled. Certainly, he dominated Australian racing for the three seasons from 1929 and, at the time, was the biggest stake winner in the British Empire.

He was bred at Timaru, on New Zealand's South Island, and was by Night Raid, a son of Radium, winner of the Goodwood and Doncaster Cups in England, out of Entreaty, a horse of no great personal distinction but with some useful family connections. The trainer, H.R. Telford, found something in the pedigrees to like and persuaded one of his owners, D. Davis, to buy him for 160 guineas at the 1927 New Zealand yearling sales, while he retained a lease on the horse.

Phar Lap's physique caused him to mature slowly, and in his first season as a two-year-old he only managed to win a six-furlong (1.20km) maiden race at Sydney's Rosehill Track from five starts, and he was no more impressive in the early part of his three-year-old season until after running a good second in the 1¼ mile (2km) Chelmsford Stakes at Randwick in mid-September. Thereafter, Phar Lap came into his own, winning his races by 10 to 30 lengths without being extended and while carrying weights that would have crippled another horse. As a three-year-old he won 13 races, including the Australian Jockey Club and Victoria Derbys. He was at his peak in the following year, winning 14 successive races including the great Melbourne Cup at Flemington when, carrying an astonishing 9st 12lb (63kg), he annihilated his opponents.

Just before the Melbourne Cup an attempt was made to shoot the horse and he was given police protection up to the start of the race. It later transpired that the incident was the work of a group of unscrupulous journalists intent on creating a story. *'Plus ça change...'*

Early in 1931 Australia's national hero established his international reputation by a record-breaking victory in the American Agua Caliente Handicap held at Tanforan in Mexico. Sixteen days later while resting at Menlo Park, California, Phar Lap died, reputedly of colic, though the mystery of his death – and there was one – remains unsolved.

It is recorded that Phar Lap's heart weighed 14½lb (6.6kg), the walls of the left ventricle being 1.7in (4.3cm) thick. Corresponding figures for other good horses were 10lb (4.5kg) and 1in (2.5cm). Dr Stewart McKay, who performed the autopsy, concluded that Phar Lap's devastating speed and stamina was attributable to this peculiarity.

THE GREAT PHAR LAP, RIDDEN BY JIM PIKE, ON THE DAY OF HIS VICTORY AT THE AUSTRALIAN JOCKEY CLUB DERBY IN 1929, BY 3½ LENGTHS AND IN A NEW RECORD TIME.

RACING WAS ESTABLISHED in Japan at the turn of the 20th century but only in comparatively recent years has it become an industry in its own right, with Japanese buyers featuring prominently at the major European sales. In common with other racing countries, Japan stages a programme of Classic races based on the British pattern.

Tokyo racecourse is 16 miles (26km) from the city at Fuchu, while 18 miles (29km) to the east of Tokyo is Nakayama at Funabashi. The course at Kyoto, the old capital of Japan, is at Yodo on specially drained ground.

The extensive Tokyo course comprises a dirt surface track as well as a turf circuit just over 1¼ miles (2km) in circumference and is over carefully undulating ground. Both a training course and an inner steeplechase course are included.

JAPAN CUP DIRT Run on Tokyo's dirt track, usually on the day before the more famous and popular turf-track Japan Cup, the Japan Cup Dirt was inaugurated in 2000. Pictured here, Hiroki Goto on Alondite rides to victory in 2006.

The major races staged at the Tokyo track are the world-famous Japan Cup, Tokyo Yuushun (Japanese Derby), the Yuushun Hinba (Japanese Oaks) and the Tennou Shou (The Emperor's Cup) for older horses.

NAKAYAMA held its first meeting in 1920 and now stages the most valuable steeplechase in Japan, the Nakayama Grand Jump. In 1956, when a new grandstand was completed, the Arima Kinen, over 1 mile 4½ furlongs (2.5km), was run for the first time. A race governed by some unusual conditions, it is a weight-for-age contest limited

to a field of 20. Ten of the runners are decided by popular vote and ten by a committee of owners, trainers, journalists and the official handicappers. Held in December, it is extremely popular, regularly setting new betting records that nowadays may approach the billion mark. The other big race staged is the Satsuki Shou (2,000 Guineas).

An undulating, right-handed turf course just over a mile (1.6km) in circumference, it incorporates the inner steeplechase course and has a dirt training track. It is an unusually wide course with a 1½-furlong (0.3km) straight. Like the Tokyo course, it puts on 40 days of racing a year.

NAKAYAMA The Japan Cup is usually staged at Tokyo racecourse, but transferred to Nakayama in 2002 while the former course was renovated. It was won by Frankie Dettori on Falbrav.

KYOTO held its first four-day meeting at Simabara in 1908 and holds only 16 days of racing a year. Nonetheless, it stages the important Japanese St Leger (the Kikuka Shou) run over 1 mile 7 furlongs (3km) in mid-November and instituted as long ago as 1938, as well as the other Group 1 race, the Queen Elizabeth II Commemorative Cup over 1½ miles (2.4km). The spring Tenno Shou, the Emperor's Cup, is held at Kyoto on the Emperor's birthday.

Kyoto is a left-handed turf track with an 8-furlong (1.6km) dirt course and an inner 'Grand Steeplechase' track of 7 furlongs (1.4km).

EAGER RACE-GOERS Tokyo racecourse attracts huge crowds and enthusiastic betting on races offering excellent prize-money.

THE INFLUENCE OF DUBAI

The major racing countries of the world – Britain, France, Italy, America and now Germany, too – have all exerted formative influences on Thoroughbred racing throughout the history of the sport, and, indeed continue to do so.

NONE, HOWEVER, can exceed the record, linking the 20th and 21st centuries, of the Maktoum family, rulers of Dubai, which is headed by the quietly charismatic HH Sheikh Mohammed bin Rashid Al Maktoum. Sheikh Mohammed owns the Darley Stud breeding operation based at the Dalham House Stud and 10 satellite farms at Newmarket and with important studs in America, Ireland, Australia, France, Japan and, of course, in Dubai itself, standing upwards of 50–60 stallions at studs worldwide.

Godolphin is the principal racing arm of Sheikh Mohammed's operation with its headquarters at the comprehensive Al Quoz complex in Dubai. Horses, including selected youngstock bought during the year, spend the mild winters here, re-grouping, as it were, after summer forays to 11 racing centres from England to Japan and Hong Kong. Summer quarters are at Newmarket at the Godolphin stables, formerly the Earls of Derby's Stanley House, and at Moulton Paddocks.

DUBAI'S RACECOURSE, at least for the moment, is the palatial Nad Al Sheba, ten minutes from the city centre and combining both grass and dirt tracks. It is exceptionally well drained and groomed continually to provide consistently good going. In March it stages the world's richest race, the $6m Dubai World Cup.

Nad Al Sheba is a world-class track but will be replaced by Sheikh Mohammed's 'racing city', Meydan, likely to be completed in time for the 2010 World Cup and set to become 'the wonder of the racing world'.

Viewed realistically, the world-embracing Maktoum enterprises, supported by infinite wealth and in every way beneficial to the industry, comes close to under-pinning Thoroughbred racing.

The only concern that might be said to rival Dubai's dominance is the Coolmore operation in Ireland (see pp.86–87) whose complement of stallions, now led by Northern Dancer's son Sadler's Wells and until recently his sons Montjeu and Galileo, is the most influential in the world.

Perhaps in recognition of Coolmore's prominence, Sheikh Mohammed has enforced a self-imposed ban on the use of Coolmore stallions and thus denied Darley the use of some exceptional bloodlines.

IN 2007, HOWEVER, Sheikh Mohammed set about rectifying the deficiency by an unprecedented, even for him, buying programme. He acquired the brilliant Derby winner, Authorized, son of Montjeu, for a reputed £10m, leasing him back to the owners Saleh Al Homaizi and Imad Al Sagar, for his racing career. Then came Teofilo, champion two-year-old of 2006 who now stands at Darley's Kildangan Stud, in Co. Kildare, Ireland. The Japanese star, Admire Moon, by End Sweep, winner of the Dubai Duty Free, was acquired at a rumoured £16m to stand at the Darley Japan Farm. Street Sense and Hard Spun, one and two in the Kentucky Derby were also bought, while at the Saratoga Yearling Sales, the Sheikh spent some $3,675,000. In addition, the five-year-old Manduro, reckoned the best horse in Europe in 2007, was brought into the Darley stallion complement to stand alongside Shirocco, winner of the Coronation Cup, at Dalham Hall. Both horses are by the German sire Monsun, owned by Baron von Ullman, a horse giving access to the very best and most successful German lines.

DUBAI (right) The palatial Nad Al Sheba racecourse with its Millennium Grandstand provides world-class facilities for both horses and spectactors, but will be replaced in 2010 by the new 'racing city' of Meydan.

NAD AL SHEBA (below) In front of the distinctive Dubai skyline, horses are put through their training paces at the Nad Al Sheba racecourse. Facilities include scrupulously maintained grass and dirt tracks.

COURSES IN THE UNITED STATES

American courses, particularly in the area of New York, whose first governor, Richard Nicolls, built a course on Long Island in 1664, developed against a background of religious and political prejudice against the sport. Churchill Downs suffered no such disadvantage, sited as it is at Louisville, in the heart of Kentucky's Blue Grass, America's horse country.

WINNER Colourfully dressed crowds cheer on the winning horse on Kentucky Oaks Day in 2007, at Churchill Downs racecourse. This prestigious Grade 1 race attracts a large and enthusiastic attendance.

CHURCHILL DOWNS was opened in 1875 and the stands, topped by symbolic twin spires, were completed 20 years later. Between 2001–05 a $121m renovation was carried out that resulted in a magnificent facility as well as a degree of controversy because the design blocked a full view of the iconic spires.

Churchill is a left-handed, oval dirt track, 1 mile (1.6km) round and with an inner turf track of ⁷/₈ mile (1.4km). The going on the dirt track is inclined to be inconsistent because, while quick drying, the surface tends to become loose and ride somewhat deep, thus prohibiting fast times. The course stages America's most famous race, the Kentucky Derby, run over 10 furlongs (2km) on the first Saturday in May, when crowds of over 140,000 are not unusual.

CHURCHILL DOWNS, 2005 The 2001–05 renovations were controversial for blocking the full view of the iconic spires, seen here at the centre of the picture. Critics complained that it was like cutting out the Statue of Liberty.

Irving S. Cobb, a homespun Kentucky character, said famously: 'Until you go to Kentucky, and with your own eyes behold the Derby, you ain't never been nowheres and you ain't never seen nothing.'

Churchill Downs also stages the prestigious Group 1 Kentucky Oaks and has hosted Flat racing's World Championships, the Breeders' Cup, on six occasions to date.

AQUEDUCT was termed 'the wonder track of Thoroughbred racing' when it was rebuilt replete with every luxury and its own subway station, 50 years ago. It has been overtaken by more prestigious courses since then but retains its association with some of America's most famous horses, and is a big favourite with the serious betting man. Situated at Jamaica, New York, it is 5 miles (8km) from Kennedy airport and 12 (19km) from Manhattan.

Aqueduct has two left-handed dirt courses of 9 furlongs (1.8km) and 8 furlongs (1.6km) circumference respectively, as well as a shorter turf track. Racing takes place six days a week between October and May, the inner dirt track being used in winter.

It was here in 1920 that the immortal Man o' War (see pp.62–63) turned an almost certain defeat into victory when conceding 18lb (8.2kg) to John P. Grier in the Dwyer Stakes, an achievement commemorated by the old furlong pole set at the entrance to the track. Kelso won 20 of his 27 Aqueduct appearances and in 1973 Secretariat paraded for the last time here.

AQUEDUCT The British-trained filly Pebbles, ridden by Pat Eddery, parades before the crowds after winning the 1985 Breeders' Cup Turf, held that year at Aqueduct racecourse.

BELMONT PARK at Elmont, New York, reconstructed some 40 years ago, is probably America's most beautiful and picturesque course and is, additionally, associated with some of the legendary horses of the American turf, including Man o' War, Citation and Secretariat, the latter commemorated by a striking sculpture.

Belmont, built by August Belmont II, breeder of Man o' War, has a 1½-mile (2.4km) left-handed dirt circuit with a 336-yard (307m) straight and two inner turf tracks. There is also a useful training track adjacent to the course. Racing takes place here May–July and September–October. The course stages an impressive number of Group 1 races both on dirt and turf, both the Man o' War Stakes 1 mile 3 furlongs (2.6km) and the 1½ mile (2.4km) Turf Classic being run on the latter.

Belmont's top attraction, however, is the historic 12 furlongs (2.4km) Belmont Stakes, the final leg of America's Triple Crown, won by horses of the calibre of Citation, Secretariat and Seattle Slew. The race, over this distance, is a severe test of stamina taking into account the unusually long back straight, the track's sweeping curves and the final, very demanding 2 furlongs (0.4km) to the finish.

PIMLICO, in Baltimore, Maryland, 40 miles (64km) from Washington DC, does not compete with Belmont in size, facilities or the number of racing days staged, which are limited to the April–May meeting. Nevertheless, it occupies a special place in the American racing scene and its peculiarly tight turns and occasional changes in the going often produce unexpected results.

PIMLICO (above) The field breaks out of the starting gates in the 2004 Preakness Stakes at Pimlico racecourse. This coveted event, named after an early winner at the course, is the second Classic race of America's Triple Crown for three-year-olds.

TRIUMPH (top left) Jerry Bailey on Saint Liam enters the winners' enclosure at Belmont Park after winning the 2005 Breeders' Cup Classic, which was staged at this course in that year. The race is one of the richest and most prestigious in the world.

BELMONT PARK (bottom left) In one of the most famous finishes ever staged at Belmont, the legendary Lester Piggott, just out of retirement, galvanises Royal Academy (left) to a stirring success in the 1990 Breeders's Cup Mile.

It is a 1-mile (1.6km) oval track of sand and loam with an inside turf track of 7 furlongs (1.4km). The first meeting at the Pimlico course was staged by the Maryland Jockey Club on 25 October 1870. Two days later the 2 mile (3.2km) Dinner Party Stakes was run and was won by a big, awkward colt named Preakness. The Jockey Club named a race after him, the distance of which was only finally settled at 9½ furlongs (1.9km) in 1925.

The Preakness was to become the second Classic of the Triple Crown for three-year-olds and carries the additional attraction of the Woodlawn Vase Trophy, the most valuable in American racing. It was created in 1860 by Tiffany & Co. and presented to the Club in 1917. There have been memorable moments in the running of the Preakness but probably none to approach Secretariat's pulverising charge that took him from last to first at the final Club House turn in 1973.

The infield at Pimlico stages sports events and music festivals, particularly popular at the Preakness meeting.

The colt Preakness raced until he was eight, when he went to England and the ownership of the Duke of Hamilton, whose temper was reputed to be worse than that of the horse. In the end the two fell out and the Duke shot Preakness, who 120 years later is immortalised in the second Classic of the American Triple Crown.

AS TRACKS GO, Keeneland is something of a Johnnie-come-lately, being not much more than 70 years old. But this is the famed Blue Grass country and the racing tradition in Kentucky has been firmly established since the late 18th century. The first meeting staged at Keeneland, by the Keeneland Association, did not, however, take place until 1936.

Keeneland lies 6 miles (10km) west of Lexington in Kentucky and has meetings in the spring and autumn. The dirt track is an 8½-furlong (1.7km) oval and there is also a 5-furlong (1km) training track.

One of the most attractive tracks in America, Keeneland is laid out with some magnificent gardens and for many years had no public address system, which some might consider a unique advantage. The race for which Keeneland is most noted is the 9 furlong (1.8km) Blue Grass Stakes run during the spring meeting and nine days before the Kentucky Derby at Churchill Downs. Winners of the Blue Grass quite frequently go on to triumph in the Derby.

A particular feature behind the stands at Keeneland is the statue of a jockey. The owner of the horse winning the Blue Grass has the right to have the statue painted in his colours until the next year.

THE FIRST RACE MEETING held at Saratoga Springs, New York, was on 15 August 1863, a month or so after General Lee's retreat from the bloody fields of Gettysburg when the American Civil War was at its height.

That such 'a great fashionable race meeting' could have been held against the background of carnage that was Gettysburg and also the war's subsequent battles, is in keeping with the 19th-century 'good-time' character of Saratoga. The town was founded on the excesses of gambling and larger-than-life gamblers like Diamond Jack Brady and John 'Bet-a-million' Gates, and founded by an Irish gangster, John Morrisey, who finished up as a US Congressman. He opened a gambling hall and built race tracks as a further dimension for large-scale betting, the last one being constructed on the site of the present course.

Modern Saratoga has long since become respectable, although without losing its raffish reputation entirely. Moreover, it stages top-class racing during its season in August.

Sited 30 miles (48km) from Albany, New York, the dirt track is a 9-furlong (1.8km) oval of sandy loam, with an inner, banked turf track and a smaller steeplechase course.

Known as 'The Graveyard of Favourites', this was the track on which America's hero Man o' War lost the only race of his career when he was beaten in 1919 by the appropriately named Upset in the Sandford Stakes in a badly run race. Eleven years later the Triple Crown winner Gallant Fox was beaten by eight lengths in the Travers Stakes by obscure 100–1 outsider Jim Dandy.

In 1973, record crowds filled the Saratoga complex to see the great Secretariat in the Whitney Stakes. He, too, followed the Saratoga tradition by running second to the unregarded Onion, who thus won the only stakes race in his unremarkable career.

KEENELAND At the heart of Kentucky's Blue Grass racing country, Keeneland racecourse, home to the Blue Grass Stakes, maintains high standards both on and off the track, and is particularly noted for its attractive gardens.

SARATOGA (above) The field starts off at a 2003 race meeting, but heavily backed riders may be feeling some trepidation: Saratoga is notorious as 'The Graveyard of Favourites', numbering among its victims such greats as Man o' War, Gallant Fox and Secretariat.

SARATOGA (left) The field thunders round the 9-furlong (1.8km) sandy loam course past the grandstands. Top-quality racing and Saratoga's raffish background as a good-time gambling town have surely encouraged generations of race-goers at this course to have a little flutter.

MAN O' WAR *An unbeatable horse*

Man o' War, known to his thousands of admirers as 'Big Red', is generally acknowledged as the greatest racehorse bred in America.

A big, fiery and impetuous horse, who was difficult to break, he was not only a charismatic individual but was also uniquely powerful with a remarkable ground-devouring action. Odds-on favourite in all his 21 races he was beaten only once, as a two-year-old at Saratoga in 1919 (see pp.60–61), and that was due to a bad start (no starting stalls in those days) and a disastrous riding error on the part of his jockey, Loftus.

He never ran in the Kentucky Derby because his owner, the eccentric Samuel D. Riddle, who idolised the horse, disapproved of the race being held so early in the season, but he won the other two races of the Triple Crown, the Preakness and the Belmont Stakes, as well as the rest of his races, without being stretched and while always giving unprecedented weights to his rivals. Only in his last race in 1920 against the older Sir Barton, winner of the 1919 Triple Crown, did he carry less weight than his opponent. In his three-year-old career he broke seven track, American or world records and was in every way regarded as unbeatable. He won the Lawrence Realisation at Belmont Park from Hoodwink by 100 lengths with his jockey, Kummer, standing in his stirrups and pulling hard against him. But many regard his finest performance as in the Dwyer Stakes at Aqueduct (see p.57) when he beat John P. Grier in an electrifying finish when conceding 18lb (8.2kg).

Man o' War was bred in 1917 by August Belmont, founder of Belmont Park. He was by Fair Play, whose grandsire Spendthrift was the son of West Australian, the inaugural winner of the English Triple Crown in 1853. His dam was Mahubah (Arabic for 'good tidings') by the English Triple Crown winner Rock Sand. Belmont, deeply involved in war work, sent his youngsters to the Saratoga sales in 1918 where Samuel Doyle Riddle bought Man o' War for $5,000.

When Man o' War retired from the track, Riddle built Faraway Stud for his favourite, restricting the number of mares sent to him. Nonetheless, as well as a group of influential daughters, he got the American Triple Crown winner, War Admiral; War Relic, heading a line of winners through the mare Relance, being also the sire of Battleship, the 1938 Grand National winner, and the smallest horse to win the race (15.2hh/1.5m); and Blockade (1929), three-time winner of the Maryland Hunt Cup.

Man o' War died in 1947 and his lying in state and funeral were attended by thousands of Americans while commentaries were broadcast on the radio. An honorary citizen of Lexington and honorary Colonel of the US Cavalry, he is buried now at the Kentucky Horse Park, where he is commemorated by Hubert Haseltine's heroic statue of America's 'mostest horse that ever was'.

MAN O' WAR REMAINS A LEGEND IN RACING FOR HIS SPECTACULAR FINISHES, RECORD-BREAKING RACES AND HIS REPUTATION AS AN UNBEATABLE HORSE.

For most people 'racehorse' is synonymous with Thoroughbred and indelibly associated with the established form of racing that has its roots in 17/18th century Europe. In reality, it is probable that racing dates from the early domestication of the horse some 6,000 years ago. Both Greeks and Romans bred horses specifically for racing a long time before the emergence of the Thoroughbred (see pp.14–17) and today there are horses other than the Thoroughbred that in their own field are just as deserving of the description 'racehorse'.

THE RACEHORSE

SECRETARIAT (above) One of a duo of horses with Kelso who dominated American racing in the 1960s and 70s, Secretariat also proved his worth at stud, being recognised as the leading broodmare sire in 1992 and siring winners of the Melbourne Cup and Preakness Stakes.

SOVIET SONG (left) A recent star on the track, Soviet Song, seen here ridden by Oscar Urbina at Royal Ascot, was the highest-rated older filly in the world in 2004 and 2005.

THE ARAB

The Arab horse is the principal progenitor of the Thoroughbred (see pp.14–17), although by no means as fast. It does not run over fences or hurdles, nor does it attract the volume of money gambled on Thoroughbred racing, and Arab racing remains largely an amateur sport.

ARAB HEAD The Arab has a distinctive dished profile, with a shield-shaped forehead known as the *jibbah*, and slightly inward-curving ears. This beautiful breed is the principal progenitor of the Thoroughbred, but is a distinctively smaller horse, usually standing at around 14.3hh (1.5m).

ARAB The high-carried tail and free, floating action make the Arab a joy to watch in movement. Although not the Thoroughbred's equal in speed, its toughness and stamina make it a natural choice for competitive endurance rides.

NONETHELESS, PURE-BRED Arabians, as well as Anglo-Arabs and part-breds, still take part in organised racing in many parts of the world. Not surprisingly, they also enjoy the supportive patronage of the rulers of Dubai throughout the range of their activities.

Before the advent of the Thoroughbred and in the formative years of its development, races involving Arabs were more about distance and stamina than otherwise and sometimes took place over a period of days! That situation is partly replicated in the modern, competitive endurance rides, a sport in which members of the Maktoum family participate enthusiastically and with considerable success.

In the past, in British India of the 19th century and the early part of the 20th, Arabs were often raced on the Flat and over fences. Indeed, races confined to pure-

breds were held at the principal meetings up to India attaining independence in 1947.

A notable Arab of the 19th century, with an awesome record, was the stallion Maidan imported to Bombay (Mumbai) from the Nejd in 1871. He raced successfully on the Flat and over fences, won the Kadir Cup, the blue riband of the dangerous sport of pigsticking, and also served as a charger. In that last capacity he took part in the relief of Suakin, marching from Port Said to Massawa and back (866 miles/1,394km) before going on to Marseilles to race over the banks in the Pau country. In England, at 20 years of age, he won three point-to-points and at 22 he won a 3-mile (5km) chase. Unhappily, he broke a leg in the following year and was put down.

Modern Arab racing has its own central body, the International Federation of Arab Horse Racing Associations (IFAHR) which was founded in Paris in 1999 with 18 founding members from Europe, the Middle East and America. While IFAHR is not a governing body in the sense of rule-making, discipline etc, it exists to foster 'co-operation between all national and international Arab Horse Racing Associations throughout the world'.

The UK authority is the Arabian Racing Organisation (ARO), formed with help from the British Arab Horse Society. It operates with the support and permission of the Jockey Club of Great Britain and the British Horseracing Board and its purpose is to regulate and promote the racing of Arabians in the UK. In pursuit of that objective the ARO stages full race days at some 15 courses with a number of single races for Arabs, Anglos and part-breds at

Thoroughbred meetings. Sprints (5–7f/1–1.4km), middle distance (1 mile–1 mile 3f/1.6–2.2km) and long distance races (12f–2 miles/2.4–3.2km) are all featured.

One particular attraction of Arab racing is that is a largely amateur sport. Jockeys are all amateurs, who get a chance to ride against professionals in handicap and group races held at Thoroughbred meetings, and so are most of the trainers. As for the spectators they are, unlike many race-goers, knowledgeable horse enthusiasts who add immeasurably to the charm and interest of Arab racing.

THE AKHAL-TEKE

Three thousand years ago the racing industry was centred
not on Newmarket, Lexington, Longchamp or Dubai, but in
and around the oases of Turkmenistan, north of Iran and east
of the Caspian Sea. These are the homelands of the Akhal-
Teke and its related breeds the Iomed and the Turkmene.

AKHAL-TEKES Although there is
little evidence to back up Russian claims that
the Akhal-Teke is a 'pure-bred', it is indisputable
that the breed resembles very closely the Horse
Type 3 postulated as a development from early
primitive horses. The common golden-metallic
dun coat colour can be seen in this herd.

DESERT HORSE As befits a horse that developed in a desert environment, the Akhal-Teke is famously heat- and drought-resistant. Its stamina is a match for that of the Arab, but its ability to cover great distances on minimal water intake sets it apart from other breeds.

AS LONG AGO AS 1000BC Ashkhabad, where today's Komsomol Stud is a major breed centre for the Akhal-Teke, was famous for its racehorses and, allowing for its much reduced influence in the modern context, remains so today. Five hundred years later, the elite 30,000 strong Bactrian guard of King Darius of Persia (522–486BC) were mounted on just such swift and enduring horses, regarded as the best obtainable.

Russian authorities, despite little or no substantive evidence, claim the Akhal-Teke is a 'pure-bred', whatever that may mean, and as old as the Arab horse. There is no way of establishing the truth of those assertions but it is certain that the Akhal-Teke approximates very closely to the Horse Type 3 postulated by leading hippologists (led by Professor J.G. Speed of Edinburgh) as a post-glacial development from the early, founding 'primitives'. These were the Asiatic Wild Horse; the Tarpan, of eastern Europe and the Ukranian steppes; and the heavy Forest or Diluvial Horse of the northern

European marshlands – which, one imagines, had very little to do with the evolution of a heat- and drought-resistant desert horse. There is a certain resemblance to the earlier Arab racing strain, the Munaghi, but whether the Munaghi influenced the development of the Akhal-Teke or the other way about is not a matter for useful conjecture.

What is certain is that the Akhal-Teke is unique among the world's equine population. It is as enduring as the Arab and capable of covering great distances on a minimal water intake; additionally, the modern Akhal-Teke goes some way towards being an all-round sports horse.

The most famous test of the breed's endurance was the ride made from Ashkhabad to Moscow in 1935. The distance involved was 2,580 miles (4,128km), 600 miles (960km) of which was over desert where water was scarcely available. Indeed, for much of the journey the horses were almost without water. That epic journey was completed in a remarkable 84 days.

NONETHELESS, it is racing that remains endemic to the Turkoman people and until comparatively recent times, training practices included the wrapping of horses in heavy felt, which certainly gave protection against the cold of desert nights, but also ensured a complete absence of surplus fat when worn in the midday sun.

Even today, horses are fed a notably high-protein/low-bulk diet. The traditional food comprised a little dried lucerne, mutton fat pellets, eggs, barley and *quatlame*, a fried dough cake.

Conformationally, the Akhal-Teke, standing around 15.2hh (1.6m), is not, by Western standards, an impressive specimen. The neck rises almost vertically from the shoulders to give a characteristically high head carriage, while the back is often long. Sickle hocks are sometimes apparent as well as narrow, but nonetheless deep, chests. The coat, however, is very fine and the skin particularly thin, a characteristic of desert-bred horses.

Coat colours are striking, especially the golden-metallic dun and the less frequent silver-metallic.

The speed of the Akhal-Teke is not comparable to that of the Thoroughbred and at one time experiments were made to introduce Thoroughbred outcrosses in an attempt to remedy the difference. Outcrossing, however, diluted the essential character of the breed and was soon discontinued. The Akhal-Teke is also bred in Kazakhstan, at Gubden in Dagestan and on a smaller scale at the Tersk Stud in the northern Caucasus.

THE QUARTER HORSE

Originating in 17th-century Virginia and neighbouring settlements on America's east coast, the Quarter Horse is the oldest all-American breed.

QUARTER HORSES English settlers on America's east coast needed a horse that could carry out all kinds of work, and, apart from its racing credentials, the versatile Quarter Horse has proved adept at transportation and farmwork, in particular cattle herding, being an unparalleled 'cow-pony'.

EARLY TITLES given to what swiftly became a highly distinctive type were the 'American Quarter Running Horse' and the more grandiose the 'Famous and Celebrated Colonial Quarter Pather', both references to the horse's racing ability over a quarter mile (0.4km). In fact, while the horse's racing potential was both encouraged and appreciated by the sporting English settlers, the Quarter Horse was used for every sort of purpose from working cattle, which it does instinctively as a sheepdog works sheep, to undertaking all sort of jobs on the farm and taking the family to church on Sundays.

The foundation for the uniquely conformed Quarter Horse was the result of crossings between the existing base stock of Spanish/Barb blood and imported English horses. The first significant importation of the latter was in 1611 when 17 stallions and mares were landed in Virginia. These represented the native 'running horse' stock, based on Spanish and Italian blood mixed with that of the swift Galloways of northern England and the renowned Irish Hobby, which was to form the seed-bed from which the Thoroughbred would evolve.

While the settlers needed a sound, versatile horse, up to any sort of work, the principal consideration in Quarter Horse breeding was the ability to sprint over short distances from a standing start. In the absence of open ground (like Newmarket Heath, for instance) horses were raced over quarter-mile stretches cut through the scrub or on paths through the plantations, or even in the village street, hence the name Quarter Horse or quarter-miler.

The horse bred to this requirement was compact, chunky and with massively developed quarters and thighs. It stood, as it does today, about 15hh (1.5m) and

is described by one American authority as 'a strongly built sprinter standing between a slender distance runner and powerfully muscled shot-putter or weight-lifter.'

By 1656 Quarter Horse racing was well established in Virginia, but with the advent of Thoroughbred racing and oval tracks the emphasis shifted to the Western states where the Quarter Horse was recognised as the world's greatest cow-pony. Indeed, it was claimed that from a flat-out gallop a Quarter Horse could 'turn on a dime and toss you back nine cents change'.

Modern Quarter Horse racing – 'short-racing' – is carried on enthusiastically at tracks throughout Texas, Arizona, Nevada and California, and at venues elsewhere in the US since the prize-money often exceeds that available in Thoroughbred racing.

In fact, the Quarter Horse register, with an entry of millions, is the largest

CONFORMATION The breed's original use as an all-purpose, versatile horse that was also capable of racing over short distances from a standing start encouraged the development of a distinctively compact and chunky horse, with well-developed quarters and thighs.

in the world with the major Quarter Horse population outside the US being in Australia.

Use has been made of a Thoroughbred outcross in the interest of developing even greater speed, but this is possibly at the risk of detracting from the characteristic explosive standing start.

The breed's two most notable foundation sires are Janus and Sir Archy. Janus is at the base of the powerful Punter line and Sir Archy, the son of the first English Derby winner, Diomed, is also connected with the American Saddlebred foundation.

GREAT RACERS

Between the two World Wars, racing in England was dominated by two men: the 17th Earl of Derby and HH The Aga Khan. The latter, leading owner on thirteen occasions, owned five Derby winners of which the best was Bahram, winner of the English Triple Crown and undefeated in nine races.

BAHRAM WAS FOALED in 1932 at the Aga Khan's stud in Co. Kildare and was by Blandford out of Friar's Daughter. Blandford was not an outstanding racehorse because of a set of doubtful joints, but he was a great champion sire of Classic horses and got four Derby winners including Bahram. Nor was Friar's Daughter, bought for 140 guineas, a great performer, winning just one minor race, but she bred seven good winners, excluding Bahram. Even more significantly, St Simon, one of the greatest racehorses and sires in Thoroughbred history, appeared three times in the first four generations of her pedigree.

Bahram won his first race, the National Breeders' Produce Stakes over 5 furlongs (1km) in 1934 and the Triple Crown and Ascot's St James's Palace Stakes in the following year. Instead of racing as a four-year-old, when he might well have sealed his reputation as a very great horse, Bahram went to stud siring three top-class horses in Big Game, the St Leger winner Turkham, and Persian Gulf.

In 1940 the Aga Khan sold Bahram as well as the other Derby winners, Blenheim and Mahmoud, to America, from whence, after five seasons he was sold to the Argentine where he died in 1956.

Bahram was not a charismatic horse and his victories were never spectacular. He was, indeed, a very idle horse by nature and described as the laziest horse he ever rode by his jockey, Freddy Fox. Conversely, his trainer Frank Butters, who had produced exceptional horses like Fairway, Colorado and the great Mahmoud, considered him the best horse he ever trained.

IN CONTRAST TO BAHRAM was a remarkable horse and possibly the fastest ever to race in England. Preceding Bahram by 20-odd years, The Tetrarch was bred by Edward Kennedy in Co. Kildare in 1911 in an effort to revive the Herod male line. His sire was the French-bred Roi Herode, an unremarkable horse but possessed of a superb racing pedigree. His dam was Vahren, a shy breeder by the Two Thousand Guineas winner, Bona Vista.

The Tetrarch was just as remarkable in appearance as in his inspired performances on the racecourse. He was described as being 'a kind of elephant grey with white and lime patches…as if someone had splashed him with a brush dipped in a bucket of whitewash'. Not surprisingly, he was nicknamed 'the Rocking Horse' and later 'the Spotted Wonder'.

Trained by Atty Perse, The Tetrarch raced only as a two-year-old, being then retired as a result of an injury. Never beaten, The Tetrarch won his seven 5-furlong (1km) and 6-furlong (1.2km) races in electrifying fashion from explosive starts, making nothing of the opposition. Only once, in the Sandown National Breeders' Produce Stakes was he nearly beaten. Impetuous as ever he seemed to get his nose through the tapes and was then badly bumped and nearly came down. Nonetheless, he won by a neck although his fans did not hide the disappointment at so tight a victory – they expected runs that pulverised the opposition.

At stud he was less than enthusiastic, getting only 130 foals in his career and being completely infertile for ten years before his death in 1935. Nevertheless, he sired three St Leger winners – Caligula, Polemarch and Salmon Trout – while transmitting his great speed to his sons Tetratema and Stefan the Great and to his brilliant daughter, 'the flying filly' Mumtaz Mahal.

Atty Perse said that 'he would never have been beaten at any distance. He was a freak and there will never be another like him.'

BAHRAM (above) Bahram arrives for the 1935 Derby, which he would go on to win, taking the Triple Crown. Despite his racing success, Bahram was retired to stud at the end of the 1935 season, and went on to sire three top-class winners: Big Game, Turkham and Persian Gulf.

THE TETRARCH (left) This remarkable horse, possibly the fastest to have ever raced in England, was also famous for his distinctive colouring, captured in this portrait. His unusual paint-splashed appearance led to the nicknames 'the Rocking Horse' and 'the Spotted Wonder'.

HYPERION, owned and bred by the 17th Earl of Derby, has been called the greatest 'little' horse of the 20th century. He was, indeed, little, standing at 15.1½hh (1.5m) when fully grown and under 15hh when he went into training, but he played a dominant role in Classic breeding. He was foaled in 1930 and had an illustrious pedigree. His sire was Gainsborough and his dam Selene, both with direct lines to St Simon. Gainsborough won the 1918 Triple Crown and Selene was winner of fifteen races and a prolific breeder.

Hyperion was a sweetly tempered horse of near perfect conformation and something of a character, but he was not easy to train because by nature he was an indolent individual. Nonetheless, he won four good races as a two-year-old and in

1933 he had five victories including the Derby and St Leger. Retiring to Lord Derby's Woodland Stud, Newmarket, in 1934, where he remained until his death in 1960, he proved himself as one of the greatest sires in Thoroughbred history and leading sire on six occasions. Among his progeny were Owen Tudor (Derby and Gold Cup winner), Sun Castle (1938 St Leger), Sun Chariot (1,000 Guineas, Oaks and St Leger in 1939), Sunstream, Gulf Stream and Aureole, all of them excellent stallions, while his daughters were important broodmares.

THE 17TH EARL OF DERBY and HH The Aga Khan are acknowledged as two of the most important owner-breeders of the last century, but just as pre-eminent

was the vastly influential Italian genius, Federico Tesio, who bred some of the world's most famous horses at his Dormello Stud on the banks of Lake Maggiore. His two great horses were Nearco and Ribot. The former is described in the Dormello stud book (a very special one designed by Prince Lubomirski, owner of the Kruszyna Stud in Poland) as being 'beautifully balanced, of perfect size and great quality. Won all his races as soon as he was asked. Not a true stayer…he won longer races by his superb class and brilliant speed.'

Foaled in 1935, he was by Lord Derby's Pharos out of Nogara, a mare by the leading sire Havresac III. She won the Italian 1,000 and 2,000 Guineas and was described as 'a first class racer from 12–

1,600m'. A brilliant broodmare, her son Nicolaus by Solario sired the 1961 Grand National Winner, Nicolaus Silver.

Nearco won his seven victories as a two-year-old and seven in his season as a three-year-old including the momentous win in the Grand Prix De Paris, with almost contemptuous ease. After the Grand Prix he was bought by Martin Benson and was sent to Beech House Stud, Newmarket, where he remained until his death in 1957. He was an outstanding success as a sire, his Classic winners

including Dante, winner of the Derby; Nimbus (2,000 Guineas and the Derby); Sayajirao; Masaka and Neasham Belle.

RIBOT was foaled at the English National Stud in 1952, his dam Romancella being on a visit to Tenerani, Ribot's sire and one of Federico Tesio's twenty Italian Derby winners, and winner of both the Queen Elizabeth Stakes at Ascot and the Goodwood Cup.

Ribot was unbeaten in 16 races, winning the Prix de l'Arc de Triomphe

twice and the Gran Premio di Milano in majestic fashion, while his win at the King George VI and Queen Elizabeth Stakes in 1956, his only race in England, was a performance of sheer class on a saturated Ascot course and desperately inconsistent going.

He was at stud in England, Italy and then, finally, at the Darby Dan Farm, Kentucky, where he died in 1972. He became one of the world's Classic sires with Arc de Triomphe winners such as Molvedo and Prince Royal II.

NEARCO (top left) Bred at Federico Tesio's famous Dormello Stud in Italy, Nearco enjoyed great success as a two-year-old and three-year-old before being retired to stand at the Beech House Stud. His winning form was passed on to many of his progeny.

HYPERION (left) The 17th Earl of Derby's superb Hyperion, seen here grazing near his trainer, George Lambton (left). Hyperion carried the bloodline of the great St Simon through both his sire and his dam, and went on to prove himself one of the greatest sires in Thoroughbred history.

RIBOT (top right) Federico Tesio's great horse Ribot is remembered for his majestic victories in races including the Prix de l'Arc de Triomphe, and for his winning progeny. His sons Raguso, Ribocco and Ribero were all winners of both the Irish Derby and Doncaster's St Leger.

LESS THAN 20 YEARS cover the foaling of three exceptional horses illustrating the global character of the Sport of Kings. They are Mahmoud, bred in France in 1933; Citation bred at Calumet Farm, Kentucky, in 1945; and Native Dancer, also foaled in Kentucky, at the Dan W. Scott Farm, Lexington, in 1950. Both Mahmoud and Native Dancer were greys.

Mahmoud, bred by the Aga Khan, was by the Aga's first Derby winner, Blenheim, out of Mah Mahal by Gainsborough out of the famous Mumtaz Mahal, who was by The Tetrarch. Not sold at the Deauville sale, he went to be trained by Frank Butters at Newmarket.

He established himself as one of the best two-year-olds of his year with victories at Newmarket, Goodwood and Doncaster, and though many doubted his ability to stay he dealt with firm ground in exemplary fashion. After a troublesome start in the 1936 Derby, Mahmoud took the lead two furlongs from home, winning easily from Taj Akbar (also owned by the Aga Khan) in a record time of 2 minutes $33^4/_5$ seconds. The going was hard and almost bare, unlike the modern carefully tended turf, and Mahmoud took full advantage of it.

Mahmoud, along with the Aga's other Derby winners, was sold, controversially, to the US in 1940 having sired Majideh, winner of the Irish 1,000 Guineas and the Irish Oaks and the dam of the Oaks winner Masaka. In America he sired many winners and some very good broodmares. He died in 1963 in Kentucky.

CITATION is commemorated by a bronze statue behind the stands at Hialeah, Florida, where he won his first race in his three-year-old season, causing him to be acclaimed with Man o' War as one of the two

NATIVE DANCER (left) The horse who brought racing into the homes of thousands, Native Dancer was an early television star. In the days of poor quality, black-and-white TV, his grey coat, along with his electrifying finishes, were an enormous advantage, all the other horses looking black and blurred.

MAHMOUD (far top left) The striking grey Mahmoud, owned by HH The Aga Khan, achieved great success as a two-year-old and went on to win the 1936 Derby in a record-setting time of 2 minutes 33⁴/₅ seconds.

CITATION (far bottom left) Citation, in the centre of the picture, on his way to winning the 1948 Kentucky Derby, ridden by Eddie Arcaro. Considered by some to be one of the greatest horses of the 20th century, along with Man o' War, he has the distinction of being the first equine dollar millionaire.

greatest American horses of the 20th century. That may be arguable but he was a winner of the American Triple Crown and the first equine dollar millionaire. He was bred at Calumet by the legendary Bull Lea out of Hydroplane, by little Hyperion out of the Oaks winner Toboggan.

Citation was not a prepossessing individual but he was unusually intelligent, very equable in temperament and very fast. He had eight wins out of nine appearances as a two-year-old and at three he won 19 races out of 20 starts, which speaks volumes for his constitution, and easily topped the earnings list.

Citation was not a success at stud and failed to found a significant dynasty, but he remains as one of the world's top racers.

NATIVE DANCER'S career coincided with the spread of television and the public was quick to make a TV idol of the 'Grey Ghost of Sagamore' who did more than any other horse, except possibly Arkle (see pp.120–21), to popularise the sport. Bred and owned by Alfred G. Vanderbilt he was by Polynesian out of Geisha. Unlike Citation, Native Dancer was an impressive horse, massively built and enormously powerful. Undefeated as a two-year-old,

he won nine races and created a record in winnings. As a three-year-old he won another nine races and another hatful of prize-money, but largely because of jockey error failed to win the Kentucky Derby. He won three races as a four-year-old but then developed foot problems and was sent to stud, where he did not quite fulfil expectations, although he sired Kauai King, winner of the 1966 Kentucky Derby and Preakness Stakes. In Europe he is remembered for the brilliant Hula Dancer and Dan Cupid, sire of the outstanding Sea-Bird, winner of the Derby and the Prix de l'Arc de Triomphe. He died in 1967.

NIJINSKY Nijinsky, ridden here by his regular jockey Lester Piggott, was an outstanding racer as a two- and three-year-old. When he died at stud at Claiborne Farm in Kentucky, he was buried between two Kentucky Derby winners, Riva Ridge and Secretariat.

NIJINSKY was bred in Ontario, Canada, by Edgar P. Taylor, and put Canada firmly on the world map as a producer of high-class Thoroughbreds and a major influence in the industry. He was by Northern Dancer, by far the best three-year-old of his year on the American continent and winner of the Kentucky Derby and the Preakness. As a stallion, Northern Dancer was even more significant, siring, for instance, Sadler's Wells, for so long a mainstay of the Coolmore enterprise. His dam was the fiery Flaming Page, a winner of Canada's Queen's Plate, from whom Nijinsky inherited his high-strung temperament. Foaled in 1967, he was sold to Charles Englehard for a record price and was then trained in Ireland by Vincent O'Brien, co-founder of Coolmore.

His career, comprising 13 races, was marked by brilliant performances. He was the champion two-year-old in England and Ireland and in the following year won the English Triple Crown (2,000 Guineas, Derby and St Leger) and was Europe's Horse of the Year in 1970. He also triumphed in the Irish Derby and was a brilliant winner of Ascot's King George VI and Queen Elizabeth Stakes. Unhappily, for whatever reason, his career ended in anticlimax. Following his failures in the Prix de l'Arc de Triomphe and the Champion Stakes he was retired to Claiborne Farm, Kentucky, where he sired Golden Fleece, winner of the Derby, and Ferdinand, victor of the Kentucky Derby as well as numerous European and Canadian champions. He died at Claiborne in 1992.

BRIGADIER GERARD and Mill Reef were both foaled in 1968, and the pair were to dominate British racing throughout their careers although a perverse providence prevented their ever meeting head-to-head other than in the 2,000 Guineas.

Brigadier Gerard was owned and bred by John Hislop, champion amateur jockey, breed expert and sporting journalist, and was scarcely 'bred in the purple'. Out of Hislop's average mare La Paiva, he was by Queen's Hussar, no more than a moderate horse. Nonetheless, trained by Dick Hern, this consummate horse won 17 races out of 18 starts, including the 2,000 Guineas in which he beat Mill Reef, already acclaimed as a potential superstar. Brigadier Gerard raced successfully as a four-year-old, retiring to the Egerton Stud following his final victory in the Champion Stakes at Newmarket. At stud he sired the 1980 St Leger winner Light Cavalry, and Vayraan, winner of the Champion Stakes, but was not otherwise notable.

MILL REEF was bred by the millionaire philanthropist and Anglophile Paul Mellon at his Rokeby Stud in Virginia. He was by Never Bend, the son of Nasrullah by Nearco, the latter being the grandsire of the great Northern Dancer and was out of the good mare Milan Mill. The little horse, just 15.2hh (1.6m), highly intelligent and much loved by his handlers, was trained by Ian Balding in Kingsclere. He won five races as a three-year-old when he established his place as a very great horse by winning the Derby, Eclipse, King George and then the Prix de l'Arc de Triomphe. After two wins as a four-year-old, he broke three bones in his near-fore while at exercise and was cared for by a devoted staff at Kingsclere. He recovered and went to stand at the National Stud, siring two Derby winners, Shirley Heights and Reference Point, and Fairy Footsteps, winner of the 1,000 Guineas.

Mill Reef died in 1986 having twice been champion sire.

BRIGADIER GERARD (above left) Despite having unremarkable breeding, Brigadier General proved to be a consummate horse, winning 17 races out of 18 starts and dominating British racing alongside Mill Reef.

MILL REEF (above right) Jockey Geoff Lewis steers the victorious Mill Reef past spectactors after the Epsom Derby, 1971. After the horse's death, Paul Mellon commissioned John Skeaping to make three bronze statues of his favourite. One is at the National Stud, one at Kingsclere and the last on the Mellons' Virginia estate.

SEA-BIRD II and Ribot were probably the two best racehorses in the 1950s–60s and the former was certainly the best of an outstanding crop of French three-year-olds in 1965, when he won the Derby in brilliant style from a strong field. He went on to win the Arc de Triomphe from the hitherto unbeaten Reliance and other fierce opponents, to confirm his reputation as a thorough stayer blessed with a phenomenal turn of speed.

Sea-Bird II was bred and owned by M Jean Ternynck, by the American-bred Dan Cupid out of Sicalade, a combination of American speed and traditional French stamina.

As a two-year-old in 1964 he had three runs and won twice, but as a three-year-old he was quite outstanding with superlative, runaway victories in all his five races. The horse was then leased for a record sum to the American breeder, John W. Galbraith. Sea-Bird II returned to France at the end of the lease and died there a year later when he was only eleven. Unhappily, he was not as great a stallion as he was a racehorse and failed to pass on his remarkable qualities to any notable progeny.

THE AMERICAN-BRED KELSO and Secretariat were the heroes of the 60s and 70s, dominating American racing in a way that is unlikely to be repeated. Kelso had the advantage, in the sense of a long racing career, of being a gelding. Born in 1957, and later gelded because of his impossible intransigence, he raced from 1959 to 1966. Nicknamed 'King Kelly', the plaque on his box at Woodstock Farm, Maryland, his home in retirement, proclaims him as 'The most durable horse in racing history' and records that he was voted Horse of the Year for a record five successive years between 1960 and 1964 and in each of those years won the Jockey Club Gold Cup. He ran in 63 races, recording 39 wins, 12 seconds and 2 third places, while amassing a world record in earnings.

Bred by M C. duPont at Claiborne Farm, Kentucky, he was by Your Host out of the unremarkable Maid of Flight, to give him lines to Hyperion, Mahmoud and Man o' War in his pedigree. In retirement he was hunted by his owner, Allaire duPont, with her Vicmead Hounds and proved to be a great mount across country.

SEA-BIRD II (top right) Pat Glennon rides to the winners' enclosure following Sea-Bird II's victory in the 1965 Derby. Although impressive as a two-year-old, it was as a three-year-old that Sea-Bird II showed his quality with outstanding victories in all of his five races.

KELSO (above) Kelso, voted Horse of the Year for a record five successive years and a dominating figure in American racing in the 60s and 70s, was the darling of thousands of American enthusiasts, although, in fact, he was never a 'nice' horse. He was, nonetheless, a very great racehorse.

SECRETARIAT, winner of the American Triple Crown in record times and winning the third leg, the Belmont Stakes, by 31 lengths, was an example of an inspired breeding plan. Born in Virginia, he was by Bold Ruler out of Somethingroyal, a potent combination. Bold Ruler was by Nasrullah, five times US leading sire, and he himself was a Preakness winner and acknowledged as the sire of the fastest, most early maturing stock in the world. He was eight times leading sire. The dam, Somethingroyal, was by Princequillo, an equable imported Irish horse of great stamina. Strains from these two Claiborne stallions were highly complementary, 'nicking' consistently to produce outstanding progeny.

Secretariat won 16 of his 21 races, including the significant Canadian International on grass. He was US Horse of the Year in 1972–73, recognised as the leading broodmare sire in 1992, and featured on a US postage stamp in 1999. Retired to Claiborne, he contracted laminitis and had to be put down at the age of 19. Among his progeny were the Melbourne Cup winner, Kingston Rule, and the Preakness and Belmont Stakes winner, Risen Star.

The autopsy after his death showed that Secretariat had an unusually large heart weighing 21lb (9.5kg), with the average being only 8½lb (4kg).

SECRETARIAT (above) The great Secretariat pictured on his farewell appearance at New York's Aqueduct racecourse in 1973, on the eve of his retirement to stud. After his death at the age of 19, statues of Secretariat were erected at Belmont Park and at the Kentucky Horse Park.

THE AGA KHAN'S SHERGAR was considered by many to be the greatest horse of the 20th century, an accolade that is by its nature notoriously impermanent. He was, however, a great horse by any criteria.

Foaled in 1978, he was by Great Nephew out of Sharmeen. Great Nephew was a good miler and a successful sire, his get including the illustrious Grundy, winner of the 1975 Derby and Irish Derby and the King George VI and Queen Elizabeth II Stakes. Shergar was not rated highly as a two-year-old but at three he was the easy

winner of the Chester Vase and became the hottest favourite for the Derby since Sir Ivor in 1966. He ran probably the greatest Derby of the century, winning by a record 10 lengths when pulling up. He took the Irish Derby in similar style and then trounced the field of older horses in the King George VI and Queen Elizabeth II Stakes. He failed in the St Leger in an uncharacteristic performance and the Aga Khan, controversially, did not enter him for the Arc. Shergar's career ended in tragedy and with unprecedented media coverage.

He was kidnapped from the Ballymany Stud in County Kildare and, it was held, killed by the IRA in February of 1983.

LAMMTARRA is also linked to tragedy, his trainer, Alex Scott, being murdered by an unbalanced stud groom in 1994.

Whether Lammtarra was truly great is difficult to assess because of his short career in which he only ran four times, albeit unbeaten. Nonetheless, as a three-year-old, trained by Saeed bin Suroor, he won an historic treble, the 'modern triple

crown' as it was termed, comprising the Derby, King George and Prix de l'Arc de Triomphe and won them all with awesome efficiency if by no great margin.

Lammtarra was bred, with an impeccable pedigree, in Kentucky in 1992 by Sheikh Maktoum of Dubai. His sire was Nijinsky (see p.78), while he was out of the Oaks winner Snow Bride. After a season at Dalham Hall Stud, Lammtarra was sold for $30m to the rapidly expanding Japanese market to stand at astronomical fees.

THE MARE OUIJA BOARD was bred and owned by the 19th Earl of Derby. Born in 2001, she is by Cape Cross out of Selection Board by Welsh Pageant, with lines to Tudor Minstrel, Court Martial, Double Deal and Alycidon.

She raced for four seasons, winning over £3m and won the Breeder's Cup Filly & Mare Turf in America in 2004 and 2006, placing her among the best race mares in history. In her career she won 10 of her 22 races, 7 of them Group 1 contests. She won the Oaks and Irish Oaks in 2004, the

Princess Royal Stakes and the Hong Kong Vase in 2005, and in 2006 the Prince of Wales's Stakes and the Nassau Stakes at Goodwood where she was given a rapturous reception after beating Alexander Goldrun in a photo-finish.

In 2004 Ouija Board was European Champion three-year-old filly and took the Eclipse award for the Outstanding Female in 2004 and 2006. She was European Horse of the Year in 2004 and 2006 and also European Champion Older Horse in 2006.

LAMMTARRA (above) Lammtarra on his way to winning the 1995 Derby. He beat Mahmoud's 1936 record time by a second and a half, albeit over a much improved surface.

SHERGAR (far left) Acclaimed as one of the greatest horses of the century after his majestic Derby performance, Shergar's promising stud career was cut short by his high-profile kidnap.

OUIJA BOARD (left) Ouija Board, pictured with her owner Lord Derby, who has written her biography. She is honoured at Lone Star Park, US, where she won a Breeders' Cup, by a handicap race bearing her name.

AUTHORIZED, sired by the Coolmore stallion Montjeu and grandson of Sadler's Wells, was out of Funsie by Saumerez, winner of the 1990 Prix de l'Arc de Triomphe, and was thus well qualified by virtue of his pedigree for an outstanding career. Trained by Peter Chapple-Hyam, who bought him as a yearling for £400,000 on behalf of the racing partners Saleh al Homaizi and Iam al Sagar, Authorized was acquired by Sheikh Mohammed's Darley studs following his impressive five-length win in the 2007 Derby when ridden by Frankie Dettori (see p.93). Like Derby winners before him, he was then targeted at Sandown's Eclipse Stakes, last won by an Epsom winner, Nashwan, in 1989. In the event Authorized was beaten in what Chapple-Hyam termed 'a mess-up' by Notnowcato, cleverly ridden by Ryan Moore. All was then focussed on the Juddmonte International at York's Ebor meeting and with Authorized, Dylan Thomas (winner of the King George) and Notnowcato in contention it became the race of the 2007 season. Authorized redeemed himself entirely, showing Dylan Thomas a clean pair of heels down to the finish and was poised for the acid test at Longchamp, the Prix de l'Arc de

AUTHORIZED Frankie Dettori rides Authorized to a five-length victory in the 2007 Epsom Derby. Following this impressive win, Authorized was bought by Sheikh Mohammed's Darley studs.

PEEPING FAWN Star filly Peeping Fawn had a highly successful 2007 season, which was originally intended to culminate in the l'Arc de Triomphe before the decision was taken to rest her.

Triomphe, where he would face a strong challenge from his old rival Dylan Thomas. It was the latter who avenged his defeat in the Juddmonte International and gave Aidan O'Brien his first win in the Arc, winning a great race in great style.

Authorized is still a very, very valuable property. If he had won the Arc…the sky would have been the limit.

PEEPING FAWN, Ballydoyle's star three-year-old filly of 2007, is the product of the Danehill–Sadler's Wells cross that is proving to be most successful. Danehill, her sire, who died in 2003, was a grandson of Northern Dancer and her dam Maryinskey is a daughter to Sadler's Wells. Peeping Fawn won the 2007 Irish Oaks, Nassau Stakes, Pretty Polly Stakes and the Yorkshire Oaks. A tough horse with a great turn of foot, she was the most brilliant filly to emerge in 2007 and was originally intended to contest the Arc de

Triomphe. However, it was decided to rest her until 2008, but injury forced her to be retired prematurely.

SOVIET SONG, the highest-rated older filly in the world in 2004 and 2005 is less classically bred but is undeniably a very good horse and a good winner to boot. She is owned by the UK's most successful racing syndicate, The Elite Racing Club, which has a 15,000 membership. Trained by James Fanshawe at Newmarket she raced as a six-year-old, winning £1,168,370 despite having such poor feet that she had to be fitted with stick-on plastic shoes. She ran 24 times over the 5 years that she was in training, winning 9 races and being placed 8 times. She is by Marju, with both Northern Dancer and Mill Reef in her sire's pedigree. The dam, Kalinka, also has a line to Northern Dancer and, on her dam's side, to Busted.

SOVIET SONG Soviet Song with jockey Jamie Spencer on the way to winning the 2006 Windsor Forest Stakes at Royal Ascot. She raced for five years before being retired to stud in 2006.

THE HOME OF CHAMPIONS

Coolmore at Fethard, Co. Tipperary, Ireland, along with Dubai, is without doubt a most potent force on the world of Thoroughbred racing. In terms of sheer size, the Coolmore operation, although impressively wide ranging, may fall short of the mighty empire created by the Maktoums. Conversely, by reason of a brilliantly planned and executed breeding policy, producing lines that are collectively the most influential in the history of the sport, Coolmore dominates the thinking and practice of the world's racing industry.

Inseparably associated with Ireland's most prominent racing family, the Magniers, it was founded by John Magnier; his father-in-law, Vincent O'Brien, probably the greatest trainer of the 20th century, and Robert Sangster, international owner and breeder and a businessman of outstanding acumen. In fairness, they were supported by the pre-eminent influence of the Canadian-bred Northern Dancer, the leading Classic stallion and the sire of Sadler's Wells, the horse responsible for a Coolmore dynasty. A good racehorse, but a sire of phenomenal importance, he has produced over 400 winners, including 22 Classic winners and was champion sire between 1990 and 2004, a position now held by his son, Danehill.

The son of Northern Dancer out of Fairy Bridge, by Bold Reason, Sadler's Wells carries the blood of Nearco, Hyperion and Mahmoud, and is the sire of Coolmore stallions such as Montjeu, who sired Authorized, the 2007 Derby winner, and Galileo, both, along with Danehill and others, producing Group 1 and Classic winners, and, indeed, seven of the last nine Derby winners.

The racing arm of the Coolmore operation is at Ballydoyle, near Cashel in Co. Tipperary where Vincent O'Brien trained so successfully for many years. Today it is under the direction of Aidan O'Brien (no relation), Ireland's champion trainer (see p.103) and producer of a succession of big race winners worldwide.

The policy of Coolmore is to acquire the best unraced yearlings at auction or to breed them at Coolmore, using almost exclusively the Northern Dancer line which has proved so outstandingly successful ever since the Canadian breeder of genius, Edgar P. Taylor, imported the English mare, Lady Angela, in foal to Nearco in 1953. She produced Nearctic, who sired Northern Dancer, sire of Nijinsky, who was trained to win the 1970 Derby, and lots more besides, by Vincent O'Brien at Ballydoyle.

MARES AND FOALS GRAZING IN THE PADDOCK AT THE HIGHLY SUCCESSFUL AND INFLUENTIAL COOLMORE STUD IN CO. TIPPERARY, IRELAND.

The essential quartet comprising Thoroughbred racing is horse, owner, trainer and the man who actually does the business, the jockey. In the early days jockeys were low down in the social scale. Today, they are respected sportsmen, many of them wealthy men, but all inexorably connected by the need to keep down to their riding weight. Flat-race jockeys weigh in at a bit above 8st (51kg) on average, while the jump jockeys' riding weight is 2st (13kg) above that.

On their retirement, many jockeys have gone on to become successful trainers, bringing on the next generation of winners.

THE RACING TEAM

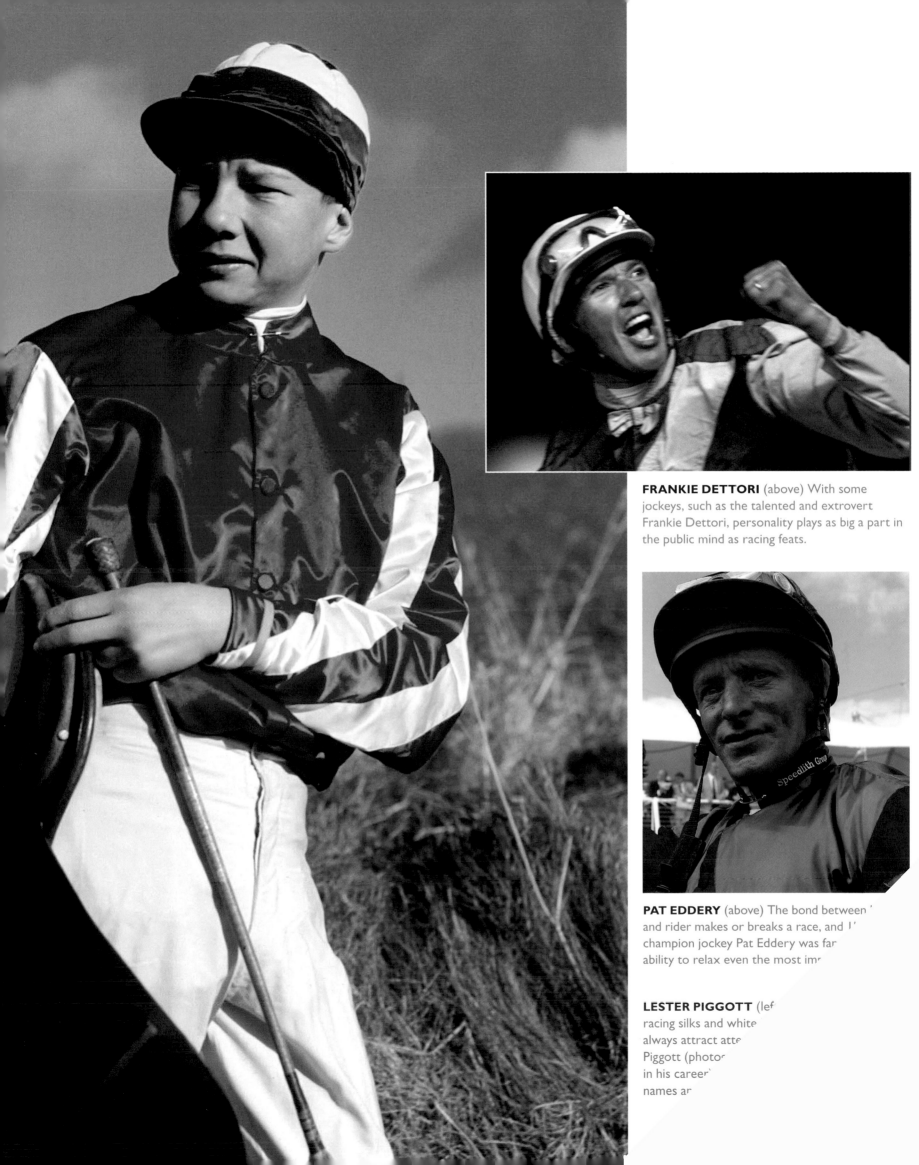

FRANKIE DETTORI (above) With some jockeys, such as the talented and extrovert Frankie Dettori, personality plays as big a part in the public mind as racing feats.

PAT EDDERY (above) The bond between ' and rider makes or breaks a race, and l' champion jockey Pat Eddery was far ability to relax even the most imr

LESTER PIGGOTT (lef
racing silks and white
always attract atte
Piggott (photo
in his career'
names ar

IN THE SADDLE

By consummate skill and by force of personality, some jockeys become as legendary as the horses they race, and often form long-lasting and successful partnerships with particular mounts. The first superstar of the Turf and a legend in his lifetime was Fred Archer (1857–86).

UNLIKE HIS MODERN counterparts, Archer rode with a long leg, sitting upright in the saddle and plied a long, whalebone whip and a pair of sharp spurs in a manner that would be unacceptable today. A powerful, forcing horseman he was also intelligent, although largely illiterate, and he was a master of tactics. Born in Cheltenham, he was the son of William Archer who won the 1858 Grand National on Little Charlie. Apprenticed to the trainer Matthew Dawson at the age of 11, his first big win was the 1872 Cesarewitch. Thereafter, largely as Lord Falmouth's retained jockey, he went on to win 2,748 races, including 21 Classics. Known as the Tin Man, he was avaricious for money but his overriding preoccupation was with his weight, which might have been a factor in his untimely death by his own hand. Archer was 5ft 10in (1.7m) tall and rode at about 8st 6lb (54kg) by dint of debilitating sweats and a strong daily purgative.

In 1884 he married Dawson's niece, Helen Rose and built Falmouth House, now demolished. The couple lost their first child and then his young wife died giving birth to a second. This personal tragedy, coupled with the relentless battle with his weight and the problems associated with remaining at the top of his profession, must have contributed to his suicide in 1886. He is buried in the Dullingham Road Cemetery.

FRED ARCHER The famous career and tragically early death of Fred Archer, a supremely intelligent and powerful rider, are commemorated in the National Museum of Racing at Newmarket.

IN COMPLETE CONTRAST to the tragic figure of Fred Archer, is the extrovert character of Willie Carson who, riding at 7st 10lb (50kg), never had Archer's weight problem.

Born at Stirling, Scotland in 1942, he was apprenticed to Middleham trainer Gerald Armstrong and won his first race in 1962, eventually riding 3,828 winners in the UK, including four Derby victories and ten other Classic races. Five times champion jockey, Willie Carson always rode with distinctive energy and great strength for so small a man, and also with an awesome determination to win that endeared him to the punters. He had the ability to read a race, judge the pace and time his challenge to the split second.

Today, Willie's infectious, cackling laugh is heard by thousands as he works as a pundit for the BBC, while standing on a box to bring him nearer to matching the height of his co-presenter Clare Balding.

Willie is also a successful breeder, running his own Minster House Stud.

Willie Carson was always a real horseman, proving himself, if any proof were needed, when he finished the last two furlongs of the 1974 Epsom Oaks riding bareback after Dibidale's saddle slipped and still finishing third, although he was later disqualified for losing his weight cloth.

WILLIE CARSON The five-time champion jockey makes his way to the start of the 2,000 Guineas. Unlike most Flat-race jockeys Willie frequently used to spend his winters in the hunting field.

ONE RIDER ABOVE ALL had dominated world racing ever since his first Derby win at the age of 18 in 1954, when he rode Never Say Die to win the premier English Classic, although he had ridden his first winner six years before that in a selling handicap at Haydock Park. Lester Piggott was born to racing, the Piggotts being prominent as jockeys and trainers for generations. Ernest Piggott won the Grand National three times in the years before World War I, and Lester's father, Keith, rode over 500 winners between the wars. His mother was Iris Rickaby from a family just as steeped in the racing tradition as the Piggotts.

Lester was simply a genius in the saddle, who lived for racing and had little time for anything outside the sport. He did not have many friends, he was aloof, perhaps because of his slight speech impediment, with a reputation for being as tight-fisted as the first of the riding greats, Fred Archer. He developed his own unique style, riding short with his seat high in the air going down to the post and he got the best from a horse, often winning with animals of moderate ability.

He rode nine Derby winners and a record twenty-nine Classic winners between 1954 and 1985. He was champion jockey 11 times, riding 4,493 winners in Britain alone.

In 1985 he retired to train at his Eve Lodge Stables and was later jailed for three years for tax offences. Released on parole the following year, he returned to race riding at the age of 54, winning among other races the Breeders' Cup Mile and then in 1992 his final Classic, the 2,000 Guineas.

LESTER PIGGOTT Indisputably great, but not outgoing, Lester Piggott, like Archer, wasted to keep his weight down, which perhaps accounts for the description 'a face like a well-kept grave'.

FRANKIE DETTORI, the best known jockey of the 21st century, does not have Lester's overwhelming racing background, although he is the son of Gianfranco Dettori, thirteen times champion Italian jockey and winner of the 2,000 Guineas in 1975 and 1976. His mother, Mara, was a circus high-wire artiste and her contribution to his remarkable skill as a rider is surely evidenced in Frankie's distinctive double-jointed, low-tuck position in the saddle and the electrifying 'flying dismounts' that so delight his fans. In contrast to Lester, Frankie is an out-and-out extrovert and showman.

Born in 1970, he rode 17 winners in Italy in 1986–87 before becoming apprenticed to Luca Cumani in Newmarket in 1985. He went on to become Sheikh Mohammed's Godolphin jockey and was the champion in 1994, 1995, 2004 and 2005. Ascot, September 1996 was a unique achievement in the annals of the sport and goes down in history as 'Frankie's Magnificent Seven', the occasion when he rode all seven winners of the day. He has won more Group 1 and Classic races around the world than any other man and looks set to break more records yet.

The only race that eluded him consistently was the greatest of them all, the Derby, and that he won on his 15th attempt in 2007, giving the Peter Chapple-Hyam trained Authorized the ride of a lifetime to finish five lengths ahead of the field. Frankie's reaction in the weighing room after the race is also a part of history. On his knees, arms held high he announced to a delighted world, 'I've won the f— race!'.

FRANKIE DETTORI In contrast to Piggott, Dettori is an extrovert crowd-pleaser, who hugely enjoyed his stint as a team captain on the long-running TV show *A Question of Sport*.

PAT EDDERY, born in 1952, was among the best half-dozen jockeys of his generation, with a remarkable knack of relaxing even the most impetuous horse, while being a master of the waiting race. The son of Jimmy Eddery, the top Irish jockey who won both the Irish Derby and the Oaks, he was apprenticed to Seamus McGrath, whose assistant trainer was Pat's uncle, Con Eddery, in 1965, transferring to 'Frenchie' Nicholson's Cheltenham yard in 1967. Eleven times champion jockey, he topped 100 winners a season from 1973–2001. He had a tally of 4,494 winners in 2002 and had he continued riding would surely have topped Sir Gordon Richards's UK total of 4,870 wins by 2005. However, he decided on retirement in 2003 to train at his Buckinghamshire stud farm.

PAT EDDERY Pat Eddery celebrates a win on Haile Selassie at Windsor in 2003, shortly before his retirement. Champion jockey 11 times, Eddery looked certain to overtake Sir Gordon Richard's UK record of wins had he continued to race.

WALTER SWINBURN A mud-splashed Walter Swinburn reflects on the race. Known for his ability to encourage a rhythmical way of going in the horses he rode, his career was sadly overshadowed by injury and the constant battle to keep his weight down.

WALTER SWINBURN was the son of a successful Irish jockey, Wally, and is remembered as the ultimate stylist, associated with great horses such as Shergar, Shahrastani and Lammtarra, winners of the Derby in 1981, 1986 and 1995 respectively. He changed his style in the 1990s and did so more successfully than some of his contemporaries. Adopting the tip-toes stance of the time and gripping with the knees at the withers, he developed a particularly rhythmical way of going in his horses that contributed materially to the overall balance.

His wins included the Arc de Triomphe, numerous Irish Classics, the King George, Gold Cup, Breeders' Cup Turf and many more. In India, where he rode regularly for R.M. Puttsanna, he won 27 Indian Classics. His career was, nonetheless, overshadowed by his constant battle to keep his riding weight and for this reason he was often limited in the rides he was able to take. In the end, indeed, he developed an eating disorder only put right by a year-long stay in a US clinic. Even more traumatic was the fall he had at the Sha Tin racecourse in Hong Kong early in 1996, the effects of which were evident until August of that year and prevented him from riding. Nonetheless, he celebrated his return by winning Baden-Baden's Grosser Preis on the Michael Stoute-trained Pilsudski later in the month. In the end it was the losing battle with his weight that compelled him to announce his retirement in April 2000. Since then he has been an informative commentator on the UK Channel 4 racing team and in 2005 took over the Buckinghamshire training stables of his father-in-law, Peter Harris.

KIEREN FALLON may at times have seemed to be racing's stormy petrel but there is no denying his brilliance in the saddle or his ability to analyse a race, while his final drive to the finishing line can be electrifying. Second in the Irish apprentice championship in 1987, he was the UK champion jockey 1997–99 and in 2001–03. Only a bad fall at Ascot prevented his being champion in 2000.

He has been stable jockey for Henry Cecil, Sir Michael Stoute and Aidan O'Brien's Ballydoyle stable.

Fallon won the Derby on Oath in 1999, Kris Kin in 2003 and North Light in 2004.

He has won the Arc de Triomphe twice, the Oaks three times, riding Ouija Board in 2004, the 1,000 Guineas four times and the 2,000 Guineas three times. He won the Irish Oaks on Ramruma in 1999 and the Irish Derby in 2005 on Michael Tabor's Hurricane Run, the world's top-ranked horse of the year.

KIEREN FALLON Kieren Fallon is pictured riding out with the string at the Ballydoyle stables, Co. Tipperary, as stable jockey. Although his career has been marred by controversy, Fallon is acknowledged as a brilliant rider with a great ability to analyse a race.

SIR GORDON RICHARDS was considered the greatest jockey of his time and in the words of trainer Noel Murless, 'one of the greatest of men'. One of a large family and without any horsey background, he was born in 1904 at Oakengates, Shropshire, the son of a miner. Brought up strictly in the Primitive Methodist chapel tradition and his complete integrity was never in doubt. He started his career when he applied for an apprenticeship with Martin Hartigan at Foxhill, where he came under the influence of his hero, Steve Donoghue. In his first season in 1925 he was champion jockey and thereafter held the title 25 times. In 1947 he rode a record 269 winners and between 1921 and 1954 rode 4,870 in Britain, another record which still stands. He won 14 English Classics, but waited 28 years before winning the Derby, on Pinza in 1953, six days after receiving his knighthood. Not a stylish jockey, he always rode with a 'swinging whip', which in some way produced perfect rhythm and maximum momentum, and he always rode to win.

He retired in 1954 to train at Ogbourne Maisey in Wiltshire, and was also racing manager for Lady Beaverbrook and. Sir Gordon died in 1986.

A GREAT AMBASSADOR for his country, Arthur 'Scobie' Breasley was a rival of Sir Gordon Richards and later stable jockey to Sir Gordon when he took up training at Ogbourne Maisey.

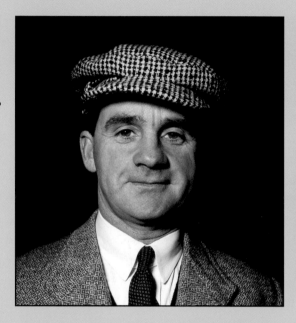

Born in Wagga Wagga, NSW, in 1914, he was nicknamed Scobie after the famous Australian trainer James Scobie. He won the Caulfield Cup in Melbourne five times and after coming to Britain in 1950 the Derby twice, when over 50 years of age, and Prix de l'Arc de Triomphe once. In England he rode over 100 winners a year between 1955 and 1964 and was champion jockey in 1957 and between 1961 and 1963. In total he rode 3,251 winners, over 1,000 in Australia.

A brilliant, stylish horseman, he made little use of the whip, his horses responding to his hands and heels, and always being beautifully balanced. He retired in 1968 to train in England, France, the US and in Barbados. On retirement in 1990 he went back to Melbourne. Liked and respected in the world of racing, he died in 2006.

STEVE DONOGHUE, who was born in Warrington in 1884, was probably the most popular jockey of his generation and not only because of his association with Brown Jack (see pp.38–39). The punters cheered him home with shouts of 'Come on Steve!' as he won every major race in the calendar and did so with dash, courage and impeccable style. He was champion jockey from 1914 to 1924 having previously ridden in France and Ireland, and won the Derby six times as well as all the other English Classics.

After his retirement from racing, he tried his hand as a breeder and trainer, but he was not a great success. However, he was undoubtedly a true horse-lover: 'I think of them as my friends,' he said, 'my greatest friends.'

Steve Donoghue died in 1945.

SIR GORDON RICHARDS (top left) Despite not coming from a horsey background, Sir Gordon Richards developed into the greatest jockey of his era, setting a record of 4,870 winners in Britain that remains unbeaten.

STEVE DONOGHUE (top right) The ever-popular Steve Donoghue is remembered for his racing dash and verve, his winning partnership with the great racehorse Brown Jack and his abiding love of horses.

ARTHUR SCOBIE BREASLEY (right) Widely admired, Breasley was the first to be inducted in the Australian Racing Hall of Fame, while the state of Victoria struck a medal in his honour that is awarded annually to the best jockey in the state.

THE TRAINERS

Answering to the owner for the wellbeing and successful preparation of the horse, the trainer plays a crucial part in the racing world. Socially, the trainer of the early 19th century was generally regarded as a sort of superior groom – which most of them were. Two men, in particular, were to change that status: Atty Persse and the Hon. George Lambton.

'ATTY', HENRY SEYMOUR PERSSE, was born in 1869, a son of the prosperous Galway Distillery family, but although a shrewd business man himself – he was director of five companies when he died in 1960 – he preferred horses to whisky and became a leading amateur rider over fences and later a Master of Foxhounds, turning to training in 1906. One of the greats trained by Atty was The Tetrarch and then his son Tetratema and his grandson Mr Jinks.

As a trainer of two-year-olds he was unsurpassed. Mentor to Sir Cecil Boyd-Rochfort, who considered him 'one of the greatest trainers in my time', he was also a fearsome old-time employer and a great bully who could be cruel to a degree.

GEORGE LAMBTON exerted perhaps an even greater influence on the social spectrum. Fifth son of the Earl of Durham, born in 1860, and educated at Eton and Trinity, where he did no work at all, he was one of the most gifted horsemen of the day, taking up training, for the Earl of

Derby, after a crashing fall at Sandown in 1892. He won the Oaks with Canterbury Pilgrim in 1896, the St Leger with Swynford in 1910 and dominated the Classics with horse like Tranquil, winner of the 1,000 Guineas and St Leger in 1923, and then in 1933 trained the immortal Hyperion to win both the Derby and the St Leger. Leading trainer in 1906, 1911 and 1912, the essentially upright Lambton campaigned relentlessly and successfully against doping, a practice introduced to Britain by the Americans, and was outright in his condemnation of partying by jockeys on the night preceding important meetings.

TWO OF THE MOST remarkable men to train in the 20th century were Fred Darling (1884–1953) and Sir Noel Murless (1910–87) and about both there was a touch of genius. The former, son of Sam Darling, who trained two exceptional Derby winners, Galtee More and Ard Patrick, began training at Kentford,

Newmarket, for Lady de Bathe (Lillie Langtry), returning after a spell in Germany to take over his father's stables at Beckhampton in 1913. Six times champion trainer, responsible for horses like Hurry On, Sun Chariot and Tudor Minstrel, he trained seven winners of the Derby and twelve of the remaining Classics. At the end of his career he bred Pinza, on whom Gordon Richards won the 1953 Derby. A man of natural authority, his horses 'stood to attention' when he made his stable rounds.

FRED DARLING was succeeded at Beckhampton by Noel Murless, who was champion trainer there in his first season and thereafter at Warren Hill, Newmarket, champion on another half-dozen occasions. He held that he had had four truly great horses in his life: Abernathy, Crepello, Petite Étoile and Gordon. However, he won a great many races with ones nearly as good: in 1967, for instance, 34 horses from Warren Hill won 60

valuable races, and a lot more money came in from a legion of placed horses. Sir Noel won 19 Classic races, 3 of them Derby wins with Crepello, St Paddy and Royal Palace who won the 2,000 Guineas in the same 1967 season. He also saddled five winners of the Oaks.

His career was notable, too, for the partnerships formed with two supreme jockeys, his friend Sir Gordon Richards and the more mercurial Lester Piggott, who was enormously successful but, perhaps, more difficult, too, on account of the suspensions his style of riding attracted at the outset of his career.

Noel Murless retired in 1976 and was knighted the following year. He was succeeded at Warren Hill by his son-in-law, Henry Cecil, stepson of Sir Cecil Boyd-Rochfort.

FRED DARLING (above) Fred Darling, pictured here in 1942 with one of King George VI's horses, Big Game, was six times champion trainer in his successful career.

GEORGE LAMBTON (top left) Coming from a privileged background, Lambton is celebrated not just for his success as a trainer but for his campaigns against doping in racing.

ATTY PERSSE (middle left) An unrivalled trainer of two-year-olds, Atty Persse was praised by his protégé Sir Cecil Boyd-Rochfort as 'one of the greatest trainers in my time'.

SIR NOEL MURLESS (bottom left) Notable trainer Sir Noel Murless (mounted) was champion trainer in his first season and thereafter on half-a-dozen further occasions.

VINCENT O'BRIEN 'The Master of Ballydoyle', Vincent O'Brien proved himself a world-class trainer of steeplechasers and Flat racers at the prestigious Irish stable. His best horse was probably the majestic Nijinsky, who won every English and Irish Classic and many other international races.

W.R. HERN Dick Hern receiving his CBE at Buckingham Palace in 1998, having been honoured with a CVO in 1980. Hern trained for the Queen at her West Isley stables for some 27 years, handling such great horses as Brigadier Gerard and Bustino.

HENRY CECIL Charismatic and popular trainer Henry Cecil made a triumphant return to top-flight racing after seven years of disappointing results when Light Shift from his stable won the 2006 Vodafone Oaks at Epsom.

KNOWN AS 'the Master of Ballydoyle', Vincent O'Brien (born 1917) is acknowledged as the greatest trainer to come out of Ireland and as outstanding as any in the history of the sport. He began training chasers at Ballydoyle in 1944 and won the Grand National in three successive years with Early Mist (1953), Royal Tan (1954) and Quare Times (1955), having already won the Cheltenham Gold Cup with the remarkable Cottage Rake in 1948, 1949 and 1950 and then once more with Knock Hard in 1953. To complete the sweep O'Brien had won the Champion Hurdle with Hatton's Grace three years running from 1949, having bought the little horse for just 18 guineas at Dublin Sales.

Turning to Flat racing, O'Brien won the Derby six times and in 1957 with Ballymoss won the Irish Derby, the English St Leger and the Prix de l'Arc de Triomphe. Nijinsky was possibly the best horse he ever trained and when O'Brien retired in 1990, he had won every English and Irish Classic, the Arc de Triomphe three times and all other major races including the Breeders' Cup Mile.

W.R. ('DICK') HERN, CVO, (1921–2002), born the son of a Somerset farmer/horse dealer, served as a cavalry officer and was an exceptional horseman who instructed at the famous Porlock Equestrian Centre. He began training in 1957 and between 1962 and 1995 had won 16 Classics,

including the St Leger 6 times and the Derby 3 times. In 1961 he went to West Ilsley where he trained for HM The Queen and managed class horses such as Brigadier Gerard and Bustino. Disabled in a hunting accident in 1984 he spent the rest of his life in a wheelchair but continued to train. Four years later he lost his position, controversially, as trainer to the Queen and then moved to Hamdan Al Maktoum's Kingwood House Stables. Dick Hern was champion trainer on four occasions.

HENRY CECIL (born 1943) took out a licence in 1969 and has been champion trainer 10 times with 4 Derby winners to his credit and 24 Classic wins in the UK with a half-dozen more abroad.

HENRIETTA KNIGHT Henrietta Knight, pictured with three-time Cheltenham Gold Cup winner Best Mate, for many years the star of the Knight stable. Training alongside her husband, former champion jockey Terry Biddlecombe, Knight has enjoyed considerable success.

Crisis point in a flamboyant and hugely successful career came when, after a disagreement, Sheikh Mohammed removed his horses from the legendary Warren Place yard. Beset by family problems, the loss of his brother David from cancer, a disease which he himself later contracted, Warren Place spent almost seven years in the wilderness before a popular and emotion-charged return to the limelight at the 2006 Derby Festival when the Cecil-trained Light Shift, owned and bred by the staunchly loyal Niarchos family, won the Vodafone Oaks from Peeping Fawn. This was Cecil's eighth Oaks winner and the reception for one of racing's best-loved and most charismatic of characters was overwhelming.

HENRIETTA KNIGHT has a stable of quality horses at West Lockinge Farm, Wantage, England, and an enviable record to match. A former biology teacher and event rider, she is married to the former champion jockey Terry Biddlecombe, who acts as assistant trainer. Much of the stable's success came from their association with Jim Lewis, owner of the legendary Best Mate, three times winner of the Cheltenham Gold Cup, and of Edredon Bleu, winner of the Champion Chase in 2000. Her stable jockey Jim Culloty always rode Best Mate to perfection. Best Mate died at Exeter in 2005 but the Knight stable continues to be a respected force in the jumping world.

SIR MICHAEL STOUTE is the establishment figure of British racing but with an unexpected background. Born in Barbados in 1945, where his father was Chief of Police, he was once a radio commentator. Now based at Freemason Lodge, Newmarket, he began training in 1972, saddling his first winner, Sandal, owned by his father, in that year. He has been champion trainer nine times, has won the Derby four times, with Shergar (1981), Shahrastani (1986), Kris Kin (2003) and North Light (2004), as well as most major races throughout the world.

SIR MICHAEL STOUTE The nine-times champion trainer celebrates another successful race. In addition to international success, in 1986 Sir Michael Stoute became the first trainer to reach the £2m mark in domestic earnings.

RACING'S EXTROVERT, entrepreneurial character is Peter Chapple-Hyam, renowned for his triumphal jig as his horses return to the winners' enclosure. Born in 1963, Chapple-Hyam, son of a Midlands greengrocer, after working with Barry Hills, Fred Rimell and Lynda Ramsden, landed on his feet by taking over Hills's training licence at Robert Sangster's Manton stables in 1991. In his first season he produced Rodrigo De Triano and Dr Devious to win the Group 1 Middle Park Stakes and Dewhurst respectively, and in the following year he sent out the former to win the 2,000 Guineas and the latter to take the Derby. Despite the steady flow of winners Chapple-Hyam left the Manton yard in 1999 for the glamour, facilities and money-making potential of Hong Kong. After five long, frustrating years he gave up an unequal struggle and came home to set about re-establishing his career, which he has done to some effect with Dutch Art, for instance, winning two Group 1 races and, of course, with the 2007 Derby winner, Authorized (see pp.84–85).

AIDaN O'BRIEN, no relation to Vincent, was the latter's successor at Ballydoyle, and controls the racing arm of the Coolmore enterprise (see pp.86–87). A record-breaking National Hunt trainer, he switched easily to the Flat and currently holds the winners' record in Ireland. A master of the big battalions, he ran eight horses in the 2007 Derby and four in the Oaks.

His first Group 1 winner was Desert King in 1995 and he won his first English Classic, the 1998 2,000 Guineas with King Of Kings. In the following year, Ballydoyle entries broke the European record for the most Group 1 winners in

the season. Among the 23 winners was the influential Galileo, who took the Derby, the King George and the Irish Derby, while Black Minnaloushe won the Irish 2,000 Guineas and the St James's Palace Stakes, with Imagine taking the Oaks and the Irish 1,000 Guineas. His second Derby win was in 2002 with High Chaparral. Today, Aidan O'Brien is firmly established as integral to the Coolmore operation and one of the world's top trainers.

JENNY PITMAN, forceful and outspoken, is an iconic and much respected member of National Hunt racing. Always patient and infinitely caring for her horses, she tolerated no nonsense with either jockeys or stable staff. Now a successful author, she trained horses of the stature of Burrough Hill Lad, Corbiere, Garrison Savannah and Royal Athlete and won the Cheltenham Gold Cup twice (Burrough Hill Lad 1981 and Garrison Savannah 1991) and the Grand National with Corbiere (1983) and Royal Athlete (1995). In addition she won the Welsh Grand National (three times), the Scottish Grand National and the Irish National, as well as the George VI Chase (Burrough Hill Lad 1984).

JENNY PITMAN (above) Much admired steeplechase trainer Jenny Pitman trained horses of the calibre of Cheltenham Gold Cup heroes Burrough Hill Lad and Grand National winner Corbiere and Royal Athlete.

PETER CHAPPLE-HYAM (top left) Flamboyant trainer Peter Chapple-Hyam with the Group 1 race-winner Dutch Art at the trainer's Newmarket stables. Hyam's biggest recent success was Authorized, winner of the 2007 Derby.

AIDAN O'BRIEN (top right) As the trainer at Ballydoyle, the racing arm of the powerful Coolmore enterprise, Aidan O'Brien works with enviable bloodlines to produce some truly great horses.

FULKE WALWYN (left) Regarded as one of the all-time great jumping trainers, Fulke Walwyn followed a brilliant career as a jump jockey with outstanding success as a trainer.

FRED WINTER (right) Another trainer who had enjoyed equal success in the saddle, Fred Winter in notable for having won the Grand National twice as a jockey and twice as a trainer.

FULKE WALWYN stands in the forefront of the jumping trainers of our time. Tim Fitzgeorge-Parker, jumping enthusiast, amateur jockey, author and respected commentator, believed him to be 'the greatest of *all* time'. A brilliant horseman, he won the 1936 Grand National on Reynoldstown but retired from the saddle after a serious fall in 1938 to take up training at Lambourn.

Fulke Walwyn was leading trainer five times, winning four Cheltenham Gold Cups, two Champion Hurdles and the Grand National in 1964 with Team Spirit. He had five victories in the King George VI Chase, a race second in importance only to the Gold Cup, and won both the Hennessy Gold Cup and the Whitbread Gold Cup on seven occasions. Possibly his most memorable victory was in the Grand Steeple-chase de Paris when in his last race the champion, Mandarin, was ridden to a head victory by Fred Winter after the bit broke in his mouth 21 fences and 3 miles (5km) before the finish.

Walwyn, notably, trained for the impossible Dorothy Paget, daughter of Lord Queenborough, and managed, probably better than any other man, to control that most odious of racing owners. He won 365

races for her including the Cheltenham Gold Cup with Mont Tremblant.

LIKE WALWYN, FRED WINTER is acclaimed as one of the greatest jumping personalities of the 20th century. As a jockey he was a legendary figure, four times champion rider and of iconic stature following his victory in the Grand Steeple-chase on Mandarin. He rode 923 winners and won the Grand National, the Champion Hurdle and the Gold Cup as both a jockey and a trainer. Indeed, he won the National twice in both roles, the Champion Hurdle four times as a jockey and three times as a trainer and the Gold Cup twice as a jockey and once as a trainer. He became a trainer in 1964 setting up at Lambourn and from there was to become champion trainer eight times, including five in a row between 1971 and 1975, sending out horses like Lanzarote, Bula, Pendil, Crisp and Killeney and the national winners Jay Trump and Anglo. For the last 16 years of his life he was confined to a wheelchair following a fall at his home, and he died in 2004.

MARTIN PIPE handed over his extensive yard at Wellington, Somerset, to his son

David after the 2006 season when he had a string of some 138 horses and had trained more winners, over 3,000, than any other trainer in the history of the jumping sport. Meticulous in monitoring the health of his horses on a scientific basis, he regularly exceeded 200 winners a season, a number never reached previously, and had a reputation for bringing out the best in moderate performers and placing them shrewdly in the races most likely to suit their abilities. He was champion trainer 11 times. He won the 1994 Grand National with Miinnehoma, the Champion Hurdle twice and more races at the Cheltenham Festival than any other trainer.

DONALD 'GINGER' McCAIN, a garage and taxi proprietor, was based at Cholmondeley, Cheshire. The archetypal, call-a-spade-a-spade Northerner, he is devoted to Aintree – 'no place like it in the world' – where he ran the fabled Red Rum, trained on the sands at Southport, to win the Grand National in 1973, 74 and 77. In 2004, he was back in the record books when Amberleigh House won the race. His son Donald took over the Cholmondeley yard in 2007.

DONALD MCCAIN (above) Pictured with the Grand National-winning Amberleigh House who he trained, Donald McCain is known for his string of Grand National wins with Red Rum in the 1970s, capped with this horse's 2004 victory.

MARTIN PIPE (right) In his long and gilded career, Martin Pipe trained more winners – over 3,000 – than any other jumping trainer in history, regularly exceeding 200 winners in a season.

STEEPLECHASING

ROBBIE POWER URGES SILVER BIRCH OVER –
OR THROUGH – A SPRUCE FENCE IN THE 2007
GRAND NATIONAL, AINTREE, ENGLAND.

National Hunt racing is the traditional winter sport of the United Kingdom, Ireland and France, meetings being held principally from autumn to spring and attracting a large, enthusiastic following.

It is claimed that the first 'match' took place in Ireland in the 18th century when, for a wager, Messrs Callaghan and Blake raced 4½ miles (7.2km) between the church steeples of Buttevant and St Leger, hence the word 'steeplechase'.

THE WINTER SPORT

BEST MATE (right) Considered by many the superstar of 21st-century steeplechasing, Best Mate won the challenging and prestigious Cheltenham Gold Cup an impressive three times.

AINTREE (far right) To fans of steeplechasing, there is no finer sight than the courage and athleticism of a horse soaring over fences. The Grand National course at Aintree has some of the most daunting fences in the sport, and demands absolute commitment from horse and rider.

THE HISTORY

Steeplechasing derives from the hunting field where in the early 19th century members would ride a 'match' against each other across country, although the sport was only of secondary interest and importance to that of foxhunting which was followed with a rare passion by its devotees. It was not until 1830 that the first organised steeplechase took place in St Albans, Hertfordshire, England.

EARLY GRAND NATIONAL (above) This painting of an early Grand National captures the thrill of the steeplechase as well as its perils: the free-running horse has obviously shed his rider over one of the fences.

GRAND NATIONAL FENCE (top) Grackle takes one of the fearsome Grand National fences in the 1931 race. The most infamous fence is probably Becher's Brook, which has caused the downfall of many a horse and rider.

THIS FIRST RACE was staged by the enterprising Thomas Coleman, formerly a stud groom and then landlord of the Chequers Tavern, which he knocked down to rebuild as the Turf Hotel, an establishment patronised by the leading sportsmen of the day. The race, under Coleman's control, was over 4 miles (6.4km) from Harlington Church to the obelisk in Wrest Park and was won by Lord Ranelagh's Wonder, ridden by a Guards officer, Capt. MacDowell. The race was run every year until 1839, when the Grand National Steeplechase was first run at Aintree, Liverpool, and won by the professional rider Jem Mason, often regarded as the best horseman in England, on Lottery, owned by a notable horse-dealer, John Elmore, whose daughter he later married.

THE GRAND NATIONAL is the most famous steeplechase in the world and its 30 formidable fences incorporated in the 4½ miles (7.2km) have their own unique character. The course has been modified over the years, the fences being built with more slope, but many of the big drops have been retained and the National continues to call for a 'specialist' horse. One of the National's best-known fences is Becher's Brook, which is jumped twice during the race. It is named after Captain Becher, son of a Norfolk farmer, who frequently rode for Thomas Coleman. He achieved immortality by falling into the Aintree brook during the first Grand National in 1839.

AINTREE and the National are a British institution, but the Mecca of the winter sport is Cheltenham, and in particular the National Hunt Festival held in March. Central to the Festival and the sport itself is the Cheltenham Gold Cup run over 3¼ miles (5.2km) with that long finish up the Cheltenham hill. First run in 1924, it made a household name of the Duchess of Westminster's Arkle (see pp.120–21), who won in 1964, 1965 and 1966. The record,

CHELTENHAM GOLD CUP (above) The highly coveted Cheltenham Gold Cup itself. This trophy is the goal of every aspiring steeplechase trainer and jockey.

CHELTENHAM GOLD CUP (top) Perhaps the most notable Cheltenham record was made in 1983 when trainer Michael Dickinson saddled the first five horses home in the Gold Cup.

however, is held by Golden Miller (see p.120) who had five consecutive wins between 1932 and 1936 and also won the National in 1934. Cheltenham's Champion Hurdle over 2 miles (3.2km) is almost as prestigious and is a special event in the winter racing calendar.

COURSES IN EUROPE

The jumping courses of Europe are dominated by Britain's Aintree and Cheltenham courses and numerous other major tracks. Indeed, the UK courses, particularly Aintree and Cheltenham, are central to the sport.

AINTREE, within the city of Liverpool, has been renovated and refurbished in recent years to provide some of the best facilities in the north of England. It is, of course, synonymous with the Grand National and for that reason alone is unique in the world of racing. The first Grand National held at Aintree was in 1839 but Aintree's first race was held in 1829 on the Flat. It was organised by William Lynn, owner of Liverpool's Waterloo Hotel, who leased the land from Lord Sefton. Lynn laid out the course and built the first Aintree grandstand. In 1949 the course was acquired by the Topham family and from that point the fortunes of Aintree were controlled by ex-Gaiety Girl Mirabel Topham who built the Mildmay course opened in 1953 within the National circuit.

After a period of vicissitudes due to the ineptitude of the property dealer who had bought the course, the Jockey Club took control in 1983 and in 2004, Amberleigh

House's year, the National meeting attracted over 150,000 spectators.

CHELTENHAM RACECOURSE at Prestbury Park was established, after years of opposition, in 1902, while the famous Gold Cup was first run in 1924 and the Champion Hurdle in 1927. Of all the race meetings in Britain, Cheltenham, with its backdrop of the Cotswold hills, is

the most English, despite the overwhelming Irish presence during Festival week. Moreover, while Aintree has a special place in the jumping sport, the Cheltenham Festival is far and away the most important jumping meeting in the world and its races are the most seriously contested.

There are two tracks at Cheltenham, the old and new, to provide good going in whatever weather conditions, and in recent years an inner, cross-country type course has been constructed that has proved very popular with both the public and participants.

Jumping ability is at a premium and the undulating ground with a long hill and a severe, uphill finish makes demands on speed and stamina that are not replicated anywhere else in the world.

CHELTENHAM (left) Horses take the water jump at Cheltenham. This testing course demands considerable stamina to cope with the undulating ground, long hill and challenging uphill finish – quite apart from the variety of fences to be jumped.

AINTREE (above) The field for the 2007 Grand National approach The Chair and The Water Jump, the last two fences on the first circuit. These fences are the only two to be bypassed on the second circuit: all the other obstacles must be tackled twice.

SANDOWN AND KEMPTON are hugely popular courses and both are easily accessible from London. Kempton has its own station on the Shepperton–Waterloo line and Sandown is adjacent to Esher, 14 miles (23km) from the capital. The tracks with their inviting, sloped fences set their own problems but they encourage faster horses and more fluent jumping.

Sandown's first meeting was in 1875, when Fred Archer (see p.90) rode a winner in torrential rain. Sandown enjoyed the patronage of the Prince of Wales and was the first wholly enclosed course in Britain,

a factor which added greatly to the family, club-type atmosphere by keeping out rowdy elements. The man chiefly responsible was Hwfa Williams, chairman and Clerk of the Course for fifty years.

The course is a right-handed oval with a steady climb of 4½ furlongs (0.9km) to the winning post. The stands, set on a hill, offer perfect viewing and the grandstand itself has every facility for the race-goer. The principal Flat race at Sandown is the Eclipse Stakes, first run in 1886 and twice won by King Edward VII. Sandown has for many years staged the Grand Military

Meeting, but today the big race over fences is the 3 miles 5 furlongs (5.8km) Bet365 Gold Cup, held in April. The great Arkle, enormously popular at Sandown, won the race in 1965 carrying 12st 7lb (79.4kg) and both Mill Reef and Desert Orchid have also been winners.

KEMPTON, at Sunbury-on-Thames, is 16 miles (26km) from London and was opened in 1878 under the aegis of S.H. Hyde, the local Conservative party agent, who leased the land six years previously. It incorporates the National

SANDOWN Fair Along (left) disputes the lead on his way to victory over the Sandown water jump. The sight of two horses battling against each other over a fence recalls the earliest days of steeplechasing, and is equally thrilling for modern spectators. Sandown, with its fast course and well-appointed facilities, is well loved in the racing world.

Hunt track on a triangular circuit of 1 mile 5 furlongs (2.6km) with a 220-yard (201m) run-in to the winning post. Unusually, the ground is entirely flat.

Early in 2006 Kempton opened its flood-lit all-weather track, a right-handed oval of 8 (1.6km) or 10 furlongs (2km) depending on whether the inner or outer bend is used. Additionally, the site hosts a weekly market as well as two antiques markets, held twice a month.

The most famous race held at Kempton is the King George VI Chase, which is held traditionally since 1947 on Boxing Day. First run in 1937 and named in honour of the new monarch, it is run over 3 miles (4.8km) and 18 fences. The first winner was Southern Hero, at 12 the oldest horse to have ever won the race. The race has grown in stature continually and is now the second most important chase in Britain, after the Cheltenham Gold Cup. Superstar Desert Orchid gave some of his most spectacular performances in the King George, winning the race a record four times. Triple Gold Cup winners Arkle and Best Mate also won the race, while Kicking King won in 2004 and 2005 and Kauto Star in 2006, 2007 and 2008.

KEMPTON Kauto Star, ridden by Ruby Walsh, wins the 2008 King George VI Chase. In addition to the triangular National Hunt course on which this race is run, since 2006 a flood-lit all-weather track has also been available at the venue.

THE BIG RACES

The Grand National no longer influences steeplechasing in the same measure as the Cheltenham Festival, but it is still the most famous race in the world and has been immortalised in thousands, or millions, of words seeking to explain its unique character and appeal. No race is so replete with dramatic incident, hard-luck stories and sometimes tragedy, too.

IT HAS BEEN WON by numerous gentleman riders, including Mr Potts who won an early 'National' on The Duke in 1837, if we count those run before 1839, and in its early years was so rough and dangerous to men and horses alike that it caused a public outcry. An English peer, Lord Manners, rode Seaman to victory in 1883 and the Hungarian Count Kinsky rode his own Zoedone to win in the following year. The American amateur Tommy Smith, winner of the Maryland Hunt Cup over timber fences, won the 1965 National with Jay Trump. An achievement, indeed. The 1884 race was won by Voluptuary who had also run in the Derby of 1881.

At the end of his career he appeared regularly on the stage of the Drury Lane Theatre to jump a small water-jump.

Edward VII, when Prince of Wales, won the race with Ambush II in 1900 and HM The Queen Mother looked certain to win with Devon Loch in 1956. Inexplicably, when Dick Francis was 50 yards from the winning post, his horse lost his stride and fell to the ground, allowing ESB to pass him.

In 1967, twenty-eight horses fell or were stopped at the twenty-third fence and the 100–1 Foinavon jumped it on his own and went on to win.

No race has ever produced a winner like Red Rum, first home in 1973 and 74, and

then the winner again in 1977 after being second in the intervening years. He typified the romance of the National like no other.

THE BLUE RIBAND of chasing, the Cheltenham Gold Cup, was first run in 1924 over the present distance of 3 miles 2½ furlongs (5.3km) and 22 fences.

By far the most successful horse in the history of the race was Golden Miller, who won five times in succession 1932–36. The Duchess of Westminster's Arkle, whose statue overlooks the Cheltenham paddock, won in 1964, 1965 and 1966. Cottage Rake completed a hat-trick in 1948–50 and Henrietta Knight produced

Best Mate to win in 2002–04. Dorothy Paget, owner of Golden Miller, won the race seven times.

THE WILDLY ECCENTRIC Count Octavian Kinsky (1813–96) of the same family as the winner of the 1893 National and a passionate fox hunter, established Europe's most unconventional steeplechase on his Hungarian estate near Pardubice, 60 miles (97km) east of Prague, in 1846 and was its first winner, despite breaking his collarbone and negotiating every sort of obstacle on a track as eccentric as himself. In 1874 the Czech Riding Club brought some sense of proportion and formality to the race. Kinsky along with Prince Thurn-Taxis was entrusted with the course and included the notorious Taxis fence, which is still jumped today, while Eastern Europe's answer to the National, the Velka Pardubicka, is known as the Grand Pardubice Steeplechase. It runs over 4½ miles (7.2km) with 31 fences and one commentator described it as resembling Hampton Court Maze. British riders won the race 13 times in the first 30 years, but it was the event rider Chris Collins who made the race known to a wider public than ever before when he won in 1973, in a record time, on the class chaser Stephen's Society. The race is fast, furious and often uncontrolled, while, in general, neither jockeys nor horses have any high degree of experience. It is, nonetheless, a steeplechase, though a far cry from Aintree, and even further from Cheltenham.

GRAND NATIONAL (top left) The field jumps Becher's Brook in the 1936 Grand National held at Aintree. The challenging fences of this course have produced some spectacular upsets, not least the 1967 race, won by the 100–1 Foinavon.

CHELTENHAM GOLD CUP (bottom left) Kauto Star takes a winning lead in the closing stages of the 2007 Cheltenham Gold Cup. The Blue Riband of steeplechasing, the Gold Cup course includes 22 fences.

GRAND PARDUBICE (above) A fallen jockey shields himself from the surrounding field at the notorious Taxis fence during the 2006 Velka Pardubice Steeplechase. This exciting race is fast, furious and often uncontrolled.

THE GREAT CHASERS

The early years of steeplechasing, when the sport had begun to acquire an acceptable social status and an aristocratic involvement that set both the tone and the rules, were notable for two exceptional horses: Lottery (born 1830) and the little grey, The Lamb (born 1862).

LOTTERY, barred from a Lincolnshire sweepstake of 25 guineas with 100 added because no horse in England would have run against him, was bred in Yorkshire out of a half-bred mare, Parthenia, by a horse also called Lottery – a situation that would not be permitted by Weatherbys today.

Lottery won a minor Flat race, under the name Chance, as a four-year-old but was slow to mature. He was purchased by John Elmore soon after and with the latter's son-in-law, the dandified Jem Mason, in the saddle and riding in a snaffle bridle, started to win races all over the country. In 1839 he won the Grand National, and in 1840 this exceptionally tough horse ran six times in a month, being walked from one course to the next. Carrying 12st (76.2kg) and upwards over 4 miles (6.4km) he won four of those races.

In his eight racing seasons Lottery won five hurdle races and sixteen steeplechases. He won his last race in 1844 after a period when a lot of courses imposed conditions that effectively barred him from running.

In retirement the most famous horse in England served first as a hunter before ending his days pulling a cart. Lottery used to express his dislike of Jem Mason in every way, but once Mason succeeded in getting into the saddle they were an unbeatable team. Lottery, for all his uncertain temper with Mason, had an endearing party trick – he would on request jump the Elmore dining table on which the luncheon was already set out without disturbing a floral decoration.

THE LAMB was not so prolific a winner, but he did win the Grand National twice, in 1868 and 1871, and was, perhaps, the most beautiful horse ever to win at Aintree or elsewhere. He was born in 1862 in Co. Limerick, Eire, by Zouave, from a good chasing family, out of a mare by Arthur, the Grand National runner-up in 1840. The grey foal was perfectly proportioned with a classic Arab head and the most gentle disposition. However, he was so small, standing at maturity under 15.2hh (1.57m), probably between 14.2–15hh (1.47–1.52m), that he was thought to be more suited as a child's pony than fitted for the rough and tumble of the racecourse. However, he did win some Flat races and went hunting, proving himself a nimble, agile performer of courage and stamina.

After winning the Kildare Hunt Plate he was bought by Lord Poulett, the sixth earl, and in the hands of George Ede, amateur jockey and cricketer, won his first National. The Lamb suffered an illness that stopped him racing for two seasons, but he won the National again in 1871 ridden by Tommy Pickernell, following Ede's death in a fall.

Sold to the German enthusiast, Baron von Oppenheim, he was fourth in the 1872 National carrying 12st 7lb (79.3kg). Entered for the Grosser Preis von Baden-Baden in September and ridden by Count Nicholas Esterhazy he struck a boggy patch of ground 100 yards from the finish and broke his leg, being put down on the spot.

LOTTERY (left) The great early chaser Lottery was slow to mature, but as a four-year-old proved himself to be a horse of exceptional toughness. In one month he raced six times, walking from one course to the next in common with the practice of the time.

THE LAMB (right) The fine head and perfect proportions of the little horse are plain to see in this contemporary portrait. He recovered from illness to win the National a second time, but had to be put down after breaking his leg in the 1872 Grosser Preis von Baden-Baden.

FOR MANY, GOLDEN MILLER will be rated the best chaser of all time, although Arkle fans would dispute the assertion.

Golden Miller was foaled in Ireland in 1927 by Goldcourt out of Miller's Pride and sold to Basil Briscoe, who trained him until 1936, for £500. Briscoe was not impressed with his purchase saying that he had wanted a potential chaser 'not a cart horse'. The Miller's first owner was Philip Carr, father of Arthur who captained England against Australia in the 1926 Test Series, and Golden Miller's first race was at Southwell in 1930 when he ran very badly. Briscoe took him hunting, which was just as disastrous, the Miller jumping badly and showing no enthusiasm to keep up with hounds. Six months later he amazed the stable by winning two good chases and his remarkable career began at that point. Sold in 1931 to the Hon. Dorothy Paget, Lord Queenborough's eccentric daughter, he won the 1932 Cheltenham Gold Cup, the first of his five consecutive victories in the Blue Riband of steeplechasing, and in 1934 he made history by becoming the first horse to complete the Gold Cup/Grand National double in the same year. But Aintree was not the Miller's course, a fact he made clear in subsequent outings.

Golden Miller won his last race in 1938, a selling chase at Birmingham, and in that year ran second to the younger Morse Code in the Gold Cup, his first defeat in the race he had made his own. From 53 starts the Miller won 29 races. Dorothy Paget retired him to The Paddocks, her

stud at Stanstead. He made guest appearances at various functions and was finally put down in 1957 at the age of 30.

TRIPLE GOLD CUP WINNER ARKLE was bred by Mary Baker at Malahow, Co. Dublin and foaled in 1957. He was by Archive, unsuccessful on the racecourse, out of Bright Cherry, who had been a good race mare. Both parents traced back to Bend Or, the 1880 Derby winner owned by the Duke of Westminster, central figure in the team that turned handicapping on its head. Arkle was owned by Anne, Duchess of Westminster, trained by the legendary Tom Dreaper, and ridden in nearly all his 35

GOLDEN MILLER (top) After a slow start to his racing career, Golden Miller went on to prove his quality and win the admiration of the public and his racing team alike. On his retirement to The Paddocks, Miss Paget ensured that he had a regular supply of apples and equally regular vet checks.

DOUBLE GLORY (above) The Hon. Dorothy Paget leads in her victorious horse, Golden Miller, after the 1934 Grand National. This completed a historic double, Golden Miller having already won the Cheltenham Gold Cup in that year.

races by the lanky Pat Taaffe. He won 27 races, never fell on a racecourse, and won all his seven races in 1962–63, won seven out of eight races in the following season, missing out under a huge weight burden in the Hennessy Gold Cup, but winning the Gold Cup at Cheltenham and the Irish Grand National. He did much the same in the following season and won all five races in 1965–66 including the King George and Gold Cup. His great rival was Mill House, the 'Big Horse', and their battles are the stuff of history with Arkle definitely asserting his superiority by beating Mill House in the 1965 Gold Cup by 28 lengths.

Arkle never ran in the Grand National. The Duchess would not let him take on the Aintree fences, 'because I adore him… he is one of the family and because he is too precious to me.'

In December 1966 Arkle broke the pedal bone in his off fore in the King George VI at Kempton. There, his leg in plaster, he held press conferences, bulletins were issued daily and he received presents, telegrams and get-well cards from admirers all over the world. In 1968 the Duchess decided her 'pet' would run no more but would be retired to her home in Co. Kildare.

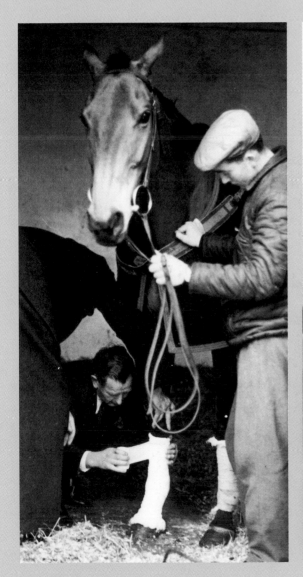

ARKLE (above left) The plaster is removed from Arkle's leg and the limb rebandaged following the pedal bone break he sustained in the 1966 King George VI Chase at Kempton. The injury prompted a wave of get-well sentiments from admirers and well-wishers of this popular horse.

SUCCESS (above right) Arkle, ridden here in 1965 by his regular jockey Pat Taaffe, had a highly successful steeplechasing career, winning 27 out of his 35 races. Due to his owner's concerns about the dangers of the Aintree fences, he never ran in the Grand National.

SIX HORSES have won the Grand National at Aintree twice, but the greatest performer of all was the three-time winner Red Rum who won in 1973, 74 and 77. Bred in Ireland in 1965 by Martin McEnery, Red Rum was out of a temperamental, 'unraceable' mare, Mared, by a local stallion, Quorum. Named using the last three letters from the names of dam and sire, Red Rum won his first race, a modest seller at Liverpool, when he was two and was in training for the next eleven years. As a hurdler Red Rum won three races from ten starts and while he made his name as an 'Aintree' horse he earned his keep by winning less prestigious races consistently. Red Rum ran five times in the National, coming second in 1975 to L'Escargot, whom he had beaten the previous year, and second to Rag Trade in 1976. To make up for that he beat Churchtown Boy by 25 lengths in 1977.

In 1974, three weeks after winning at Aintree, this extraordinarily resilient horse won the Scottish National at Ayr, an achievement marked by the erection of a statue in the paddock.

Success came despite the fact that in 1972, after a busy season, Red Rum developed pedalostitis, a serious foot inflammation causing acute lameness. Patched up he went to Doncaster Sales where he was bought for 6,000 guineas by Donald McCain for 84-year-old millionaire, Noel le Mare, for whom he was to achieve the cherished ambition of winning the National, not just once but three times. The astute McCain (see p.104) trained on the beach at Southport and made full use of the therapeutic qualities of sea-water on less-than-perfect legs and feet. In the 1973 National, Red Rum beat Crisp by three-quarters of a length and in a record 9 minutes 1.9 seconds: 20 seconds faster than Golden Miller's 1934 time.

He ran in 18 chases between 1974 and 76, winning twice and being placed seven times before winning his third National in 1977. However, just before the 1978 National, he developed a hairline fracture in the foot and was retired to take up a new career as a celebrity, appearing at races and charity events. He died in 1995.

MILL HOUSE would almost certainly have been the outstanding chaser of his time had he not raced in the same era as Arkle. Owned by Bill Gollings, who bought him for a reputed £7,500, he was highly regarded by the experts and adored by an enthusiastic public. 'There hangs about Mill House,' wrote Ivor Herbert, '...the trappings of Greek tragedy,' in which the principal actor was the immortal Arkle, who beat 'the Big Horse' into the ground in successive Gold Cups at Cheltenham.

Mill House was a big horse and could use his weight to blunder through a fence successfully. He was a great galloper and an impressive jumper, but his legs were suspect and he always wore protective bandages. Nonetheless, but for Arkle, he would have won probably three Gold Cups and the same number of King George VI Chases. As it transpired, he won the 1963 Gold Cup and three valuable chases besides and won the Hennessy Gold Cup, the King George and Sandown's Gainsborough Chase in 1964. He was second in the Gold Cup twice and won his last race, the Whitbread (now Bet365) Gold Cup, in 1966.

Bred by the Lawlors of Naas, Co. Kildare in 1957, he was by King Hal, grandson of Blandford and Pharos, out of the Lawlors' Nas na Riogh who had won eight races and was a useful broodmare.

Mill House, his legs and perhaps his heart having given up, was retired after a fall in the 1968 Whitbread Gold Cup.

MILL HOUSE (above) Jockey G.W. Robinson on Mill House at Newbury racecourse in 1963. The imposing physique of 'the Big Horse' is clear to see, as are the bandages habitually used to protect his suspect legs.

RED RUM (right) Red Rum's unmatched three triumphs in the Grand National secures his place in history. He is buried at the winning post of Aintree's National Course, while a life-size bronze in the paddock area commemorates his memory.

A SUPERSTAR of steeplechasing in the 21st century was the supremely talented Best Mate produced by Henrietta Knight's West Lockinge team: Jim Lewis, his owner; Terry Biddlecombe, Knight's husband and assistant trainer; and jockey, Jim Culloty.

Bred in Ireland in 1995, Best Mate was by Un Desperado out of Katday. Henrietta Knight found him in 1999 at a point-to-point at Lismore and was so impressed that she had persuaded Jim Lewis to buy him within a couple of days.

After a succession of good wins over hurdles Best Mate made his chasing debut at Exeter in 2000 and then won the Independent Novices Chase at Cheltenham by 18 lengths, and Sandown's Scilly Isles Chase by 13 lengths.

In 2002, with Jim Culloty up, Best Mate won his first Cheltenham Gold Cup, and ridden by Tony McCoy, because of Culloty's suspension, was an impressive winner of the King George VI Chase at Kempton. Wearing his owner's red-and-blue Aston Villa stripe colours Best Mate again won the Gold Cup in both 2003 and 2004, creating a remarkable record and ensuring his position as a crowd-pulling favourite.

A burst blood vessel prevented Best Mate from contesting the Gold Cup in 2005, a race which on his form he might have won as convincingly as in previous years. He made his return to racing in the Haldon Gold Cup at Exeter in November 2005 when the mid-week meeting attracted a crowd of over 5,000, most of whom had come to see Best Mate. Under Paul Carberry, he was well placed early on but his jockey, sensing something was wrong, pulled him up before the final fence and dismounted. Best Mate's legs buckled and he went down with a cardiac arrest and died.

He had won 15 races, raised huge sums for charity and inspired the Best Mate Anthem. It consisted of singing the words

'Best Mate' to the tune of Amazing Grace and was led and encouraged by Jim Lewis.

WITHOUT DOUBT the most exciting horse in the early years of the century, if not always for the right reasons, is the brilliant French-bred horse Kauto Star, nicknamed 'L'Extraterrestial' in his native country. (In Britain, on account of his early reckless jumping, he earned himself the title of the 'White Knuckle Ride'.)

He has won 17 of his 30 races up to January 2009, winning over £1.5m in prize-money, and was the highest-rated staying chaser since Desert Orchid until his stablemate Master Minded took over the mantle in 2008. Bought by Clive Smith in 2004 for £280,000, he won the Tingle Creek Chase in the 2005–06 season but in 2006–07 he had six wins from six runs when, as a seven-year-old, he won the Cheltenham Gold Cup, ridden by Ruby Walsh, as well as the Betfair Chase, Tingle Creek and King George. As a result, Kauto Star won his connections a £1m bonus from Betfair for winning the Betfair, King George and the Gold Cup in one season.

The horse is trained by champion trainer Paul Nicholls, formerly a jump jockey who twice won Newbury's Hennessy Gold Cup.

BEST MATE (left) Best Mate ridden by Jim Culloty jumps the last fence to take the Cheltenham Gold Cup, a race he won three times. The superstar of 21st-century steeplechasing, Best Mate's career ended in tragedy when he died of a cardiac arrest during the 2005 Haldon Gold Cup.

KAUTO STAR (above) Mick Fitzgerald rides Kauto Star to victory in the 2005 Tingle Creek Chase at Sandown. Kauto Star's successes have earned £1.5 in prize-money, and his rivalry with stablemate Denman, who beat him in the 2008 Cheltenham Gold Cup, thrills race-goers.

PARTNERSHIP (top right) Champion trainer Paul Nicholls with Kauto Star at his Manor Farm Stables, Ditcheat, Somerset. Nicholls, formerly a jump jockey who twice won Newbury's Hennessy Gold Cup, dominates jumping like no trainer before him.

DESERT ORCHID *The legend*

The strikingly handsome and charismatic grey horse, Desert Orchid, 'Dessie' to his myriad friends and admirers, along with Golden Miller, Mill House, Arkle and Red Rum, is an indisputable part of the steeplechasing legend, enjoying in his career the affection and adulation of the racing public.

Dessie was bred by the Burridge family at their Leicester home in 1979. His dam was Flower Child, daughter of Grey Orchid, a high-couraged mare with a streak of wildness, who James Burridge contrived to hunt with some success. Put to the Hunters' Improvement Society's premium stallion, Brother, she produced Flower Child, who was just as wild and self-willed.

Flower Child ran in novice chases, winning twice and being placed 10 times out of 19 starts. After careful study and following the maxim of breeding for speed, Burridge put her to Grey Mirage, a fair miler on the Flat, with a modest stud fee of £350. The result was Desert Orchid, who inherited the colour and some of the 'character' of his antecedents.

The spectacular grey coat was certainly a factor that endeared Dessie to his fans, but it was his independant character, his courage, his obvious joy in racing and the flamboyance of his soaring leaps that ensured his huge popularity amongst the general public.

Dessie won six out of eight starts in the 1983–84 season and, in 1986, he won his first King George VI Chase at Kempton on Boxing Day ridden by Simon Sherwood, who with Richard Dunwoody was his regular partner. He won the Kempton showpiece four times, the last in 1990, and always to rapturous applause, being mobbed by the crowds on his victorious return to the paddock.

His best season was 1988–89 when, after winning the King George, he took the Cheltenham Gold Cup – the ultimate prize. He won it in atrocious weather conditions, battling up the Cheltenham hill to beat Yahoo by one-and-a-half lengths, and confirming trainer David Elsworth's confidence in his grey wonder-horse. Quite simply, Cheltenham's record crowd went mad that day.

Dessie won 34 races out of 70 in his career and prize-money of £654,066. He was retired in 1991 but continued to earn large sums of money for charity while remaining a firm favourite with his adoring public.

He died peacefully in his box on 13 November 2006 and is commemorated by a life-size statue at Kempton Park, the racecourse that he made his own.

THE STRIKING DESERT ORCHID, RIDDEN BY REGULAR JOCKEY RICHARD DUNWOODY. DESERT ORCHID IS REMEMBERED BY RACING FANS FOR HIS SOARING LEAPS AND OBVIOUS DELIGHT IN RACING, AS WELL AS HIS CONSIDERABLE SUCCESS.

JUMP JOCKEYS

A vital part of the jumping team, jump jockeys require excellent riding skills and courage to tackle daunting fences. They are typically heavier than Flat-race jockeys, weighing in at over 10st (64kg). Jockeys are noticeably more articulate than most other sportsmen, and some, indeed, are capable of putting pen to paper very effectively.

LORD OAKSEY (right) Riding as an amateur amongst professionals, Lord Oaksey was a successful and respected jockey, who just missed out on victory in the 1963 Grand National. He went on to forge a second career as an admired racing correspondent and television presenter, bringing his love for the sport to a wide audience.

JOHN LAWRENCE, now Lord Oaksey, who rode as an amateur on level terms with the professionals, was a highly respected racing journalist, the *Daily Telegraph* correspondent for many years, and for a long time a key television commentator and presenter.

Riding Carrickbeg, he finished second in the 1963 Grand National after seeming to have the race won when leading comfortably at the 'elbow'. As it was, both horse and jockey had nothing left when challenged by Ayala, ridden by a very determined 19-year-old, Pat Buckley, and they were beaten by three-quarters of a length.

DICK FRANCIS, who had seemed a certain winner of the 1956 Grand National when riding the Queen Mother's Devon Loch, has since 1962 become a highly successful and prolific author of detective novels with a racing background and is still turning them out.

JOHN FRANCOME, seven times National Hunt champion jockey, has to be seen as one of the sport's most skilful horsemen and one of the most successful. In 1984 he rode his 1,036th winner and during his career won a total of 1,138 races. He never won the National, he was third and second respectively in 1979 and 1980, but he won the Cheltenham Gold Cup, the Champion Hurdle, the Welsh National, the Hennessy Gold Cup and the King George VI Chase twice.

He came to racing via the Pony Club and showjumping, winning a gold medal at the European Championships and being a member of the British Junior showjumping team. He began his racing career with Fred Winter, to whom he was apprenticed at 16 years old. Retiring in 1985, he was awarded the MBE in the following year and began to establish himself as a TV commentator/presenter and as an author. His first book, *Born Lucky*, was published in 1985, since when he has written over 20 thrillers.

PETER SCUDAMORE, as the son of Grand National-winning rider Michael Scudamore, was born to be a jockey, but he developed into one of the finest National Hunt riders of all time. Linked through his career with great trainers David Nicholson, Fred Winter and Martin Pipe, he retired in April 1993 as the rider with most wins in jumping history up to that point, his 1,677 total including two victories in the Champion Hurdle. Of his winners, 972 were saddled by Pipe, testament to a close working relationship.

It was with Pipe that Scudamore broke a new record seemingly every season, his success in no small part down to his exceptional ability to judge pace on front-running horses. Since leaving the saddle, Scudamore has established himself as an assistant trainer, journalist and broadcaster, while his son Tom has provided perfect symmetry by taking up the position of stable jockey to Pipe's son and successor David.

DICK FRANCIS Jockey to HM The Queen Mother for four years, Dick Francis missed out on almost certain success in the 1956 Grand National when her horse inexplicably fell.

JOHN FRANCOME Well known today for his TV commentary and his popular thrillers, Francome is also rightly celebrated as a highly successful National Hunt jump jockey.

PETER SCUDAMORE A frequent record breaker during his time in the saddle, Scudamore had ridden more winners than any other jump jockey when he quit in April 1993.

RICHARD DUNWOODY retired in 1999 as a result of injuries sustained in falls, but by then he had become a near-iconic figure in the sport. He was completely dedicated to racing and makes that abundantly clear in his autobiography, *Obsessed*. Until he was overtaken by Tony McCoy in 2002, he had won the most races over jumps in the UK, an astonishing 1,699, as well as 175 in Ireland and was champion jockey on three occasions from 1992 to 1995.

He won his first Grand National in 1986 on West Tip and his second in 1994 on the Martin Pipe-trained Miinnehoma, owned by the comedian Freddie Star. Of course, he was also the final partner of Desert Orchid (see pp.126–27), winning the King George VI Chase twice, in 1989 and 1990, on the redoubtable grey horse. In 1995 and 1996 he won the race again on Gordon Richards's One Man. His only win in the Cheltenham Gold Cup

RICHARD DUNWOODY No one who saw him race or has read his autobiography could doubt Richard Dunwoody's dedication to jump racing. Outside racing he has been a football agent, he took part in the 2003 Polar Challenge to the North Pole and ran in the 2004 London Marathon.

CARL LLEWELLYN Carl Llewellyn celebrates winning the Coral Welsh National at Chepstow on Bindaree in 2003. His ability to ride at a true 10st (64kg), including saddle and equipment, has put him at a distinct advantage over heavier colleagues.

was in 1988 on Charter Party, although he notched up 18 Cheltenham Festival winners between 1985 and 1998. On Highland Bud, Dunwoody won two Breeders' Cup Chases in 1989 and 1992.

Constantly seeking to improve his performance, Richard Dunwoody, who was tall for a jockey, became one of the strongest finishers in the sport and developed an individual and unmistakable style over fences.

IN HIS CAREER, Carl Llewellyn was among the top jump jockeys. A stylish, intelligent horseman, he was able to adapt to every sort of horse. Brought up in Pembrokeshire in a farming background, his interest in racing was encouraged by his father, a keen point-to-point rider. He was apprenticed to Stan Mellor and rode for trainers Jim Old and Capt. Tim Forster before becoming regular jockey for Nigel Twiston-Davies.

Initially, winners were not much in evidence, but in 1986 he won his first race on Starjestic at Wolverhampton and in the following year he scored 44 wins. Carl Llewellyn rode over 500 winners and has two Grand National victories to his credit, Party Politics in 1992 and the Twiston-Davies-trained Earth Summit in 1998.

His great advantage was being to be able to ride at a true 10st (64kg), including saddle and equipment, to which end he used his own specially devised diet. Carl Llewellyn now trains at Lambourn.

IN 2002, PAUL CARBERRY became the first man in Ireland since Charlie Swan to ride over a century of winners. His father, Tommy, was one of Ireland's great jockeys winning the Cheltenham Gold Cup three times and the 1975 Grand National when he rode L'Escargot.

Paul learned his job hunting, showjumping and point-to-pointing in Ireland and is a stylish champion jockey. He has had five winners at Cheltenham and in 1999 won the Grand National on Bobbyjo, trained by his father.

PAUL CARBERRY Irish jockey Paul Carberry has enjoyed considerable racing success, being the first to equal Charlie Swan's 1996–97 record of over a century of winners. A prestigious win came in 1999 when he rode Bobbyjo to victory in the Grand National.

that the pundits proclaimed him the finest National Hunt jockey of all time. By January 2009, he had ridden 2,900 British jumps winners, over 1,000 more than any man in the history of the sport.

'A.P.', now intent upon riding over 200 winners every season, is not only enormously strong physically but is driven by an overriding determination to win. He has dominated the sport like no other rider and in the 2007–08 season took the jockey championship for the 13th time. At the end of the 2003–04 season McCoy and Martin Pipe parted company and 'A.P.' joined Jonjo O'Neill's stable at Jackdaws Castle, Gloucestershire, and has, additionally, taken on a regular tipster column for the *Daily Telegraph* racing team.

AS TALENTED AS 'A.P.' IS RUBY WALSH, the brilliant horseman who is regular jockey to leading jump trainer, Paul Nicholls, at Manor Farm Stables, Shepton Mallet. Ruby rode Kauto Star, the horse of the year (see p.125), to win the 2006 King George VI Chase and the 2007 Cheltenham Gold Cup.

Ruby (short for Rupert) takes his name from grandfather Walsh, the first of the family to set up the training yard outside Dublin. His father, Ted Walsh, encouraged by Rupert Walsh, became a very successful amateur jockey in Ireland, but has done even better as a trainer in his own right, sending Papillon to Aintree to win the 2000 Grand National, ridden, of course, by his son Ruby. Five years later, Ruby won the National again on Hedgehunter.

Ruby has a special affinity with the Cheltenham track, the scene of some of his greatest successes. It was there that he won the Irish Independent Arkle Challenge Trophy in 2003 on Azertyuiop and then in the following year rode the same horse to win the Queen Mother Champion Chase. In 2008, he won the same race on the brilliant Master Minded.

Although tall for a jockey (5ft 10in/1.8m) he keeps to a riding weight of 10st (64 kg). He has broken both legs, his wrist and hip in the falls that are an inevitable part of the jump jockey's life.

A.P. MCCOY (ANTHONY PETER) is widely acknowledge as the greatest jump jockey of all time, a tribute to his ability to bring home the winners; more accurately, he is described as a phenomenon. He has been crowned champion jockey every year since 1996 and overturned every record. Born in Co. Antrim, he came to England in 1994 as conditional jockey to Toby Balding, promptly heading the 'conditional' (equivalent of newcomers) championship with 74 wins. Thereafter his success rate has been extraordinary and unprecedented. He rode 1,000 winners in record time, beating Dunwoody's record, and in the 2003–04 season reached the magical 2,000 winners when he rode Magical Bailiwick at Wincanton. McCoy has won every big race in the book, except the National, and when riding for Martin Pipe was so consistently successful, sometimes on moderate horses,

A.P. MCCOY (above) The enormously talented and successful A.P. McCoy is regularly champion jump jockey and has broken every record going for winners. Driven by an overriding will to succeed and gifted with remarkable skills, he has dominated the sport like no other.

RUBY WALSH (right) Ruby Walsh celebrates his win with Kauto Star in the 2007 Cheltenham Gold Cup. He has enjoyed particular success at Cheltenham, including winning the Irish Independent Arkle Challenge Trophy and the Queen Mother Champion Chase.

POINT-TO-POINT

Amateur steeplechasing, point-to-point racing, is confined to the UK and Ireland. It is run under the aegis of the British Horseracing Authority but organised otherwise by recognised Hunts or, in some instances, regiments or clubs.

THE SEASON is from December to June and there are over 200 fixtures, at all of which betting facilities are available with either Tote or bookie. A condition of entry is that horses must have been 'fairly hunted' and have a certificate to that effect from the Masters of the Hunt.

The revenue obtained from the point-to-point is a major source of income for most Hunts and to attract the largest number of spectators most fixtures are held over weekends. There are usually six to eight races on a point-to-point card, open to both men and women, and run over oval, built-up courses similar to the professional steeplechase. The majority of races are over 3 miles (4.8km) with a minimum of 18 fences to be jumped. There are, nonetheless, some longer races, over 4 miles (6.4km), while the longest is the Grimthorpe Cup over 4½ miles (7.2km) held by the Middleton Hunt in Yorkshire.

The most prestigious of the point-to-point races is the Worcestershire Hunt's Lady Dudley Challenge Cup, first run as long ago as 1898 and regarded as the Blue Riband of the amateur sport.

A members' race, confined to Hunt members and subscribers, is always included on the card, as well as a Ladies' Race.

Point-to-point racing represents an important nursery for steeplechasers and, of course, encourages young jockeys in race-riding. Ex-chasers, no longer capable of winning under professional rules, are

POINT-TO-POINT Riders compete for the lead in a Whittington Point-to-Point steeplechase in Lancashire. In recent times, the point-to-point meeting has also included pony racing, encouraging younger riders to get involved in the sport

NORTH HEREFORD (above) The field takes a fence in a point-to-point organised by the North Hereford Hunt. Amateur steeplechases provide a vital seed-bed for horses and jockeys aspiring to race professionally.

WORCESTERSHIRE (below) Sam Waley-Cohen celebrates victory on Irilut in the prestigious 2007 Lady Dudley Challenge Cup at Chaddesley Corbett, Worcestershire.

evident at most meetings and provide their owners and jockeys with a way into the sport. Otherwise, many horses start their chasing careers in point-to-points. Big winners, like Ad Hoc, the Whitbread Gold Cup winner in 2001, and the even more successful See More Business, winner of the 1999 Cheltenham Gold Cup and the King George VI Chase in both 1997 and 1999 are notable examples, along with stars like Teeton Mill; Cool Dawn, another Gold Cup winner; and, of course, the immortal Best Mate (see p.124) who began his racing career point-to-pointing in Ireland. Similarly, most of our chasing jockeys came to the professional sport after gaining experience over point-to-point tracks.

The first point-to-point is claimed to be the race run by the Worcestershire in March 1836, three years before the accepted date for the National, and was restricted to Hunt members who, not unreasonably, rode their hunters in the clothes they wore to hunt meets, red coat and all. Indeed, up to the 1930s hunting dress was still worn, particularly in the members' races.

The value of the point-to-point to the encouragement of horse breeding, steeplechasing and the overall rural economy is of obvious importance, but its continuing charm is in the intimate, go-as-you-please atmosphere, which would not exist without the sport of hunting.

HARNESS RACING

A DRIVER CELEBRATES HIS VICTORY IN
A HARNESS RACE AT THE HIPPODROME
DE VINCENNES, NEAR PARIS, FRANCE.

Over 1,400 years before the Christian era, Kikkulis, Master of the Horse to the Hittite King Sepululiamus, produced a detailed manual for the training of chariot horses. Later in time the Romans developed lightweight, skeletal vehicles and racing was a national sport in both Greece and Rome. In the United States, modern harness racing attracts huge audiences of over 30 million and offers prize-money equivalent to that offered on the Flat. The sport is second only to Thoroughbred racing in popularity and is highly organised through Europe and Australia.

AN ANCIENT SPORT

ST MORITZ Teams race specially adapted sleigh-sulkies at the famous 'White Turf' race meeting held on a frozen lake. Racing on ice was the norm for harness racing in much of Europe and Scandinavia until the 20th century.

HARNESS RACING Hugely popular worldwide, and nowhere more so than in the United States, the sport of harness racing is a thrilling spectacle that attracts big betting money.

SPECTACLE With its specialist equipment and a fanatical following by the betting public, the ancient sport of harness racing is going strong in the modern era.

THE HISTORY

Chariot racing flourished well into the Byzantine Empire and continued into the 12th century, far eclipsing in organisation and popularity any ridden sport that existed. Its modern descendants are the harness-racing sports of trotting and pacing, each dominated by specialised breeds.

FRENCH TROTTING RACE (above) This 1900s painting shows the excitement of the sport. The introduction of the bike-wheel racing sulky, invented in 1892, substantially increased spreed.

TROTTING (top) Trotting races, where horses use the conventional diagonal trot, are the most common form of harness race in Europe, Scandinavia and Russia.

PACING (right) Teams competing in a pacing race, with hobbles encouraging the desired gait. Pacing horses, whose legs move in parallel, reign supreme in US harness racing.

FLAT RACING AND CHASING
centred upon the development of the
English Thoroughbred and, similarly,
the trotting sport and that confined to the
faster pacers – whose legs move in lateral
pairs, as opposed to the conventional
diagonal trot pace – are founded on the
development of specific breeds, in
particular the American Standardbred
(see pp.144–45), at whose roots are the
renowned Norfolk Trotters or Roadsters,
capable of carrying heavy men over 60
miles (97km) or more at speeds of up to
16–17mph (25–27kph) and over less than
perfect going. From these horses developed
the Hackney, the world's most impressive
harness horse. Early records of the Hackney
Horse Society, founded in 1883, quote
the achievements of some remarkable
Trotters. Bellfounder, for instance, with
a line to Eclipse, trotted 2 miles (3km) in
six minutes. Velocity, his dam, regularly
trotted 16 miles (25km) in an hour.
Moreover, these horses, the trotting wing
of the early Thoroughbred dynasties,

underpin the unique and exceptionally
tough French Trotter (see pp.152–53).

THE DEVELOPMENT of modern
harness racing begins in the 19th century
and is conveniently divided into racing at
the conventional diagonal trot and racing
at the pacing gait. The former is generally
preferred in Europe, Scandinavia and
Russia, and France continues to race
trotters under saddle as well as in harness.
Races for both trotters and pacers are held
in most countries although nowhere do
the two compete against the other.
Surprisingly, perhaps, harness racing is
not carried out on any large scale in the
UK and Eire. There are tracks, of course,
especially in the northwest of England
and it is popular in some parts of Wales.
Conversely, in Australia and New Zealand
trotting is very much a national pastime.

In the United States the pacing horse
reigns supreme. The first stud book, *The
American Trotting Register*, was published
in 1871 and the term Standardbred was

introduced eight years later when a set of
qualifications was drawn up governing
entry into the Register. The original
'standard', from which the American
Standardbred horse takes its name, was
based on speed, horses being required
to cover 1 mile (1.6km) in 2 minutes
30 seconds, a figure subsequently reduced
substantially as increased speeds were
achieved as a result of technical
innovations: the bike-wheel sulky, for
instance (improved in the 1970s) and
the mobile starting gate. Improvements
to the former resulted in a rise in recorded
two-minute miles from 685 in 1974 to
1,849 in 1976. The first trotter (not pacer)
to go a mile in under two minutes was
Lou Dillon who did 1.58.5 in 1903.
Niatross was the first sub-1.50 pacer, a
record achieved in 1980. Pacers are less
prone to 'break' the gait than trotters.
Should a horse break it is obliged to move
over to the side and the race is lost – a
big consideration when heavy betting
is a feature of the sport.

AMERICA – HOME OF THE PACER

The pacing gait, found predominantly in the Standardbred, forms a large part of American harness racing and has resulted in highly specialised harness (hobbles and protective boots, for example), some complicated bitting arrangements and the emergence of sophisticated shoeing techniques.

TWENTY YEARS AGO, there were more than 70 major raceways of standard design, all left-handed, oval in shape and including all-weather surfaces and flood-lighting, for evening racing has been the norm ever since it was introduced at the Roosevelt Raceway, Long Island, NY, in 1940. The mobile starting gate was also a Roosevelt first, making its appearance in 1946. Principal among the raceways is Meadowlands at East Rutherford, New Jersey. Opened in 1976 it stages some of the most valuable races with prize-money that runs into millions of dollars, money that is not unusual in the harness sport.

FOLLOWING the Flat-racing practice, harness racing has its Classics and the renowned Triple Crown, for both trotters and pacers.
  The trotting Triple Crown comprises the Hambletonian at Meadowlands, the Yonkers Trot at Yonkers Raceway, New York State, and the Kentucky Futurity at Lexington's prestigious Red Mile Raceway which has been a racing centre since 1875. All the trotting Triple Crown winners returned sub-two-minute times.
  The pacing equivalents are the Cane Futurity (Yonkers), the Little Brown Jug (Delaware, Ohio) and the Messenger Stakes (Roosevelt). The pacing Triple Crown dates from 1956. Winners of the pacing Blue Riband, all returning sub-two-minute times, include the pioneering Adios Butler and the legendary Bret

Hanover, product of the Hanover Show Farms, the largest and most successful Standardbred breeding operation in the world. Bret Hanover achieved 35 consecutive victories and was a brilliantly successful sire.

Niatross, winner of the Crown in 1980 was the first sub-1.50 performer, returning a time of 1.49.1 at the Red Mile in that year.

Less than 20 years ago prize-money had reached staggering proportions. John Campbell, the sport's highest earning driver of all time, won $6,391,003 at one meeting in 1988 and by the end of 1989 had brought his 18-year-old career total to the enormous sum of $79,862,806, which can be multiplied several times to correlate with present-day values.

Most American raceways stage at least 50 meetings a year – a sure indication of the sport's popularity – and some have more than 200 meetings!

Harness racing continues all the year round. In addition to the big pari-mutual courses there are also numerous county fair raceways holding meetings during the days of the fair.

MOBILE STARTING GATE (left) The opening stage of a harness race, with the mobile starting gate accelerating away in front of the field. This type of gate, first introduced at the Roosevelt Raceway, Long Island, NY, in 1940, revolutionised the way races were run.

RED MILE (above) Teams race at the famous Red Mile Raceway in Lexington, Kentucky. The track, which was opened in 1975, is the second-oldest harness-racing track in the United States, and is the venue for the Kentucky Futurity, third leg of the trotting Triple Crown.

THE AMERICAN STANDARDBRED

Without a doubt, the American Standardbred is the world's foremost harness racer. In its own country the Standardbred is as valuable as a top-class Thoroughbred. The name derives from the practice of establishing a speed standard for entry into the Standardbred Register.

HAMBLETONIAN
Acknowledged as the main influence in the Standardbred bloodline, Hambletonian, owned by William Rysdyk, was by no means a beautiful horse, but was an extremely powerful one. Descended from Bellfounder on his maternal side, with links to Norfolk Roadsters, and the influential Messenger through his sire, Hambletonian sired 1,335 offspring to found the Standardbred breed.

THE BREED was founded in the late 18th century from an English Thoroughbred called Messenger, since when it has contributed materially to almost all the European trotting breeds. Messenger, by Mambrino out of a Turf mare, was imported from England in 1788 after a successful career on the Flat. In common with all the early Thoroughbreds he had trotting connections to the revered, quintessentially English, Norfolk Roadster. His pedigree in Vol. 1 of the *General Stud Book* shows crosses to all three of the founding Oriental sires, particularly the Godolphin (see p.15). Messenger spent 20 years at stud in Pennsylvania, New York and New Jersey. Messenger never raced in harness but his sire, Mambrino, did trot, his owner, Lord Grosvenor, once wagering 1,000 guineas that he would trot 14 miles (23km) to the hour. Messenger was bred to every sort of mare including Morgans and, importantly, the now extinct Canadian and Narraganset Pacers, descended from Europe's 'ambling' (a show pace) horses.

These horses came from English and Spanish strains that paced naturally. The Morgan features through its founding sire Justin Morgan and the Standardbred also owes something to another early trotting strain, the Clays. But it is Messenger, through his closely in-bred descendant Hambletonian 10, whose influence is paramount in the Standardbred.

Foaled in 1849, Hambletonian sired 1,335 offspring between 1851–75 and is accepted as the breed's foundation sire. Nearly all Standardbreds descend from him through his sons: George Wiles (1856), Dictator (1836), Happy Medium (1863) and Electioneer (1868). Hambletonian's dam was closely in-bred to Messenger and inherited the trotting ability from Bellfounder, of Norfolk Roadster blood. Hambletonian never raced and was certainly a less refined specimen than the Thoroughbred: even today Standardbreds are nicknamed 'jug-heads' because of their plain appearance. He was, nonetheless, very powerfully built, measuring 15.1¼hh

STANDARDBRED An American Standardbred in a trotting race at Red Mile, KY. Power, strong limbs, sound feet and straight action are essential qualities of a good harness racer.

(1.55m) at the wither and 15.3¼hh (1.60m) at the croup that allowed for enormous thrust from the quarters.

TODAY'S STANDARDBRED is equally powerful with a notably high croup. The limbs are exceptionally strong and the feet absolutely sound to allow for the effects of racing at speed. The action, of necessity, must be dead straight, to prevent injury from a blow from one leg to another. Similarly, hock joints and the hind leg overall must be conformed correctly. The average height of the breed is 15.3½hh (1.61m). The breed's first sub-two-minute miler was the pacer, Star Pointer, who clocked 1.59.25 at Readville, Massachusetts, in 1897. Perhaps the best of the American Standardbreds are those raised in the Blue Grass paddocks of Kentucky.

CARDIGAN BAY *The $1m pacer*

The Standardbred Cardigan Bay, reckoned by many to be the greatest ever harness racer, was bred in New Zealand at Sandy and Davy Todd's Mataura Stud in the province of Southland, that area of New Zealand which is the equivalent of America's Kentucky. Born in 1956, he came from a racing background of solid worth. His sire was Hal Tryax, who was to become a proven and important stallion, and his dam was the useful performer Colwyn Bay, which suggests that somewhere there was a Welsh connection, if only a tenuous one. Colwyn Bay is a seaside town on the north coast of North Wales and Cardigan Bay is the sheltered water embraced by the Llyn Peninsula that faces over the sea to Ireland. Moreover, when 'Cardy' required a six-month quarantine period on his way home from America, it was spent in North Wales on Lord Langford's Bodrhyddan estate.

They gelded Cardy early because of his 'coltish' temperament and he was, indeed, not an easy horse to train, becoming unmanageable if any other horse was ahead of him; moreover, he suffered a variety of injuries in his career.

Once these problems were overcome, Cardy raced triumphant in New Zealand, Australia and America, his great stride and bigger heart winning 80 races for him between 1960 and 1968 and amassing prize-money of over $1m, worth 10 times that today. Over a mile, he ran 1.56.5 in his home country and beat every record in Australia and America. In 1970, the New Zealand Post Office stamped his claim to fame by issuing postage stamps commemorating his career.

THE GREAT CARDIGAN BAY IN HARNESS. HE WAS THE FIRST PACER TO BREAK THE $1 MILLION MARK IN EARNINGS, MATCHING THE FEAT WITH RECORD-BREAKING TIMES AND THRILLING RACES.

RACING EQUIPMENT – ITS INFLUENCE

In the first half of the 19th century, trotters were harnessed to sulkies mounted on a pair of enormous wheels; the harness was very light but no protective boots were worn. In 1892 the bike-wheel sulky was invented. Low and light, it substantially reduced racing times.

HIGH-WHEEL SULKY The sulkies used in the first part of the 19th century were high-wheeled vehicles, similar to sporting gigs. As the equipment slimmed down, so the speeds racing horses could attain improved.

HARNESS AND TACK A variety of specialised tack and equipment – such as hobbles, overchecks, Murphy blinds and shadow rolls – is used to help ensure the safety and performance of the harness-racing team.

BIKE-WHEEL SULKIES Today's lightweight racing sulkies are a far cry from the original large-wheeled carriages. Improvements in design in the 1970s saw a dramatic rise in recorded two-minute miles.

THE BIKE-WHEEL SULKY was improved upon in the mid 1970s by an American engineer, Joe King, who made the sulky of steel instead of wood while straightening and shortening the shafts. The new sulky resulted in a spectacular rise in the number of recorded two-minute miles from 685 in 1974 to 1,849 in 1976.

As great an innovation was the introduction in 1946 at the Roosevelt Raceway of the mobile starting gate, the equivalent of Thoroughbred racing's starting stalls. It ensured a fair, level start and was welcomed by the betting punters – a powerful force in such a lucrative sport. It is made of a pair of retractable wings set on a truck. With the wings extended the full width of the track the truck is driven in front of the horse to the start line. Here, it accelerates, closes the wings and pulls away, leaving the raceway open to the line of horses.

SOPHISTICATED EQUIPMENT, designed to optimise the horse's performance, was in general use before the advent of the starting gate, while the practice of specialised shoeing was well developed. Hobbles are used on pacers to help maintain the lateral gait and their exact fit is critical to the performance. Pacers, however, are a spooky lot and can shy violently at real or imagined objects. To counteract that behavioural pattern a 'shadow roll' is fitted across the nose and just below the eyes and a system of bitting has evolved that is unique to the harness racer and is largely designed to keep the head straight. To that end, side-poles may be used, fitted to an exact length from the head to the saddle. Alternatively, a Murphy blind may be used and is less cumbersome. Alternatively, open harness bridles, i.e. not fitted with a Murphy blind or blinkers that only allow free vision

when the head is held straight, are used. It is a prime requirement to keep the head absolutely straight. If bent to one side or the other maximum speed is much reduced and the horse may strike a leg and sustain serious injury. The legs are, indeed, always well protected from the coronet up to knees and hocks and horses frequently wear a bell boot over the hoof.

An overcheck, from poll to saddle, is always an essential piece of equipment and prevents the head being lowered under an acceptable level as well as increasing control. The harness racer's wardrobe will also include a variety of martingales and nosebands, many of the figure-of-eight type.

Harness is made of either light leather or, increasingly, of plastic or web.

The production of the successful harness racer is a matter of great skill and meticulous attention to detail.

TROTTING – IN EUROPE, SCANDINAVIA AND RUSSIA

Harness racing is a featured sport in several European countries, including Germany, Denmark, Italy and the Netherlands, but France can claim to have the greatest trotting tradition tracing from the 19th century.

MOSCOW A trotting race at the famous Moscow Hippodrome. This course, founded in 1834, stages regular weekend and mid-week meetings, and is regarded as an important testing ground for Russian Trotters (see pp.154–55), the majority of which are bred in the Moscow area.

STOCKHOLM The French team of driver Christophe Gallier and horse Jag de Bellouet celebrate victory in the 2006 Elitloppet trotting race at the Solvalla racetrack outside Stockholm. Harness racing is extremely popular in Sweden, and for a long time was conducted on frozen lakes, a practice still seen in some winter resorts.

VINCENNES Teams compete for position at the famous Hippodrome de Vincennes, near Paris. Noted for its unique downhill start and uphill finish, the course proves a testing challenge for the trotters and their drivers.

TROTTING RACING IN FRANCE is based on the French Trotter (see pp.152–53), using the diagonal trotting pace that is general in Europe, and races are run both under saddle and in harness. The first races for ridden horses were held at the Champs de Mars, Paris, in 1806 and the first raceway was built at Cherbourg in the 1830s. There are now over 30 tracks in France, headed by the Hippodrome de Vincennes, the equivalent of Flat racing's Longchamp. Over 1,000 races are run annually on this unique track, which instead of being flat has a downhill start and a testing uphill finish. Trotting is also a year-round sport at Enghien, Caen and Cagnes-sur-Mer. However, no racing for pacers is held in France and that is the case generally throughout the continent. The premier French ridden race is the Prix de Cornulier and the top driven race the Prix d'Amérique, both held at Vincennes and carrying prize-money to match Thoroughbred racing.

IF ANYTHING, trotting is even more popular in Sweden, where the sport attracts bigger crowds than football and generates an annual turnover of billions including the heavy betting revenue. Upwards of 10,000 races are held annually at the principal tracks of Stockholm, Gothenburg and Malmo. Sweden and Norway have two distinct trotting horses: the warmbloods strongly influenced by American blood, and a coldblood strain that is the equivalent in prestige. In the late 19th century it was common practice to race on frozen lakes in winter. Indeed, land tracks appeared later in Sweden than in Norway, Finland and Denmark. The first major land track to be built was at the turn of the 19th century at Jagresro in Malmo. Following the legislation of the Tote in the 1920s, raceways were constructed all over the country to service the national sport. The most famous is probably Solvalla, near Stockholm, venue for the prestigious Elitloppet trotting race

In Russia, harness racing is a very popular and well-supported sport, and regular race meetings take place in the impressive Moscow Hippodrome. As is more usual outside America, most races are for diagonal trotters rather than pacers.

FRENCH TROTTERS

The sport of trotting has been established in France since the early 19th century, and the French Trotter has been recognised as a breed since 1922. The French Trotter is unique in that he is raced both in harness and under saddle, and he has also been influential in the development of the Selle Français sports horse.

FRENCH TROTTER This handsome specimen is typical of the impressive build of the French Trotter, with his well-sloped shoulders, muscular, sloping hindquarters and powerful hocks. The challenging racetrack at the Hippodrome de Vincennes demands a powerful and strong horse.

THE FIRST purpose-built raceway for trotters was developed in Cherbourg in 1836 and Normandy horse breeders quickly set about producing a horse suitable for this increasingly popular sport. They imported English Thoroughbreds and Norfolk Roadsters to cross with their native mares. Some of the most influential sires included The Norfolk Phenomenum (a Norfolk Roadster), the half-bred stallion Young Rattler and the Thoroughbred stallion Heir of Linne. But with the American Standardbred seeming to be the ultimate trotter, the French then introduced Standardbred bloodlines to further upgrade their stock. In 1937 the stud book was closed to non-French horses, although more recently it has been reopened to allow in a very select number of Standardbred crosses.

Much credit is given to a young French officer, Ephrem Houel, who returned from America to France in the early 1830s and brought with him a host of ideas on breeding, stable management and training methods which he used to develop and improve the French Trotter. One of the most influential and successful sires was Fuschia, an English half-bred stallion. He was foaled in 1883 and sired over 400 trotters, and 100 of his own sons also sired winners.

THE ENTHUSIASM IN FRANCE for ridden as well as harness trotters (10 per cent of French trotting races are under saddle) has helped preserve the unique qualities of the French Trotter breed. That, and the uniquely testing racetrack at the Hippodrome de Vincennes (the leading

TROTTING French Trotters race using the conventional diagonal trotting gait, as this individual demonstrates. Careful breeding and strict selection processes have help to preserve the quality and character of this breed.

French track) with its severe, uphill finishing straight, have contributed to the need for a very strongly built, powerful trotter, which historically has more size and scope about it than the Standardbred or Russian Trotter (see pp.154–55).

The French Trotter is an impressively built horse, usually standing approximately 16.2hh (1.67m) and is primarily bay, brown or chestnut. The Thoroughbred influence is seen in the handsome, quality head, but the source of his power and propulsion is found in the well-sloped shoulders, and the muscular, sloping hindquarters with their immensely powerful hocks. He has a very good temperament generally and this has made him popular as a riding and competition horse also. Breeding for soundness and longevity has not been overlooked either and many of the breed race successfully right through to the age of 10.

About 10,000 foals are born to the breed each year in France and a strict selection process sees only the very best making it on to the racecourse. The others find work as riding and competition horses. In fact, two Olympic showjumping champions were bred by the same French Trotter broodmare: Halla in 1956 and Jappeloup in 1988.

The breeding and promotion of French Trotters is supported by the Société du Cheval Français and it has been successful in spreading the popularity of the breed not just throughout France, but also throughout the whole of Europe. In France alone there are over 18,000 French Trotters registered to race each year.

THE ORLOV TROTTER

The Orlov Trotter is Russia's most famous horse breed and before the predominance of the American Standardbred, the Orlov was renowned as the fastest harness horse in Europe. The Orlov has great stamina and strength as well as being a very attractive horse to look at. The more modern Russian Trotter was produced as an answer to the competitive dominance of the Standardbred.

THE ORLOV TROTTER was named after its creator, Count A.G. Orlov (1737–1807) who was determined to produce a Russian-bred carriage horse that would be suited to the arduous conditions that existed at the time – the severe climate, the poor conditions of the roads, and the vast distances that had to be travelled.

Count Orlov established the Krenovsky Stud on a huge tract of land in central Russia that had been gifted to him by Catherine the Great. He worked on a massive scale, keeping as many as 3,000 horses at stud whilst he established the breed. He bred Arab stallions (the most influential being the grey Smetanka) to European mares and kept meticulous breeding and performance records. Smetanka sired Polkan I and he in turn sired the Orlov's foundation stallion, Bars I, born in 1784. Throughout most of the 19th century the Orlov Trotter excelled as the fastest harness horse in Europe; his strength and beauty found him in demand as a carriage horse also. The Orlov was also widely used to upgrade many other Russian breeds.

BY THE END of the 19th century the Orlov was proving inferior in racing terms to the American Standardbred and it was inevitable that Standardbred bloodlines would be used on the Orlov in the pursuit of greater speed. This produced the Russian Trotter, but the on-going trend to add more and more American blood to the mix has greatly diluted the original characteristics.

ORLOV TROTTERS Young Orlov Trotters at a Moscow state stud. Due to a preference for the faster Standardbreds and Russian Trotters, Orlov numbers fell in the 20th century.

ORLOV TROTTER (above) The Orlov Trotter is a generally larger and more elegant horse than the Standardbred. The Arabian influence from the stallion Smetanka means that many Orlovs have grey colouring.

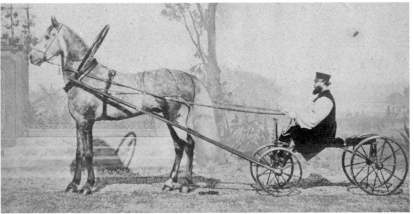

RUSSIAN TROTTER (left) This light four-wheeled carriage is drawn by an early example of a Russian Trotter. The breed was developed by crossing Orlov Trotters with American Standardbred lines, in the hope of matching the superior speed of the latter horses. As more and more American blood has been added, Russian Trotters have moved further away from the original type.

INDEX

CREDITS

Studio Cactus would like to thank Debby Sly for her invaluable contribution to the project, along with the British Horseracing Authority. Special thanks to Liz Ampairee and the wonderful Richard Dunwoody. Special thanks, too, to Elwyn's dear friend John Pawsey, Julie Thomas and Elwyn's beloved wife Mary, who helped to see this project through to the end as Elwyn would have wished. In addition, thanks to Sharon Rudd for design work; Jennifer Close for editorial work; Anne Plume for proofreading; Penelope Kent for indexing; and Sian Lloyd for picture research. Many thanks to the team at the AA, especially Mic Cady and Paul Mitchell. Special thanks to George Selwyn, Dubai Racing Club, The National Reddings Museum and The National Horse Racing Museum. Finally, thanks to Elywn Hartley Edwards, a most remarkable man who is sorely missed.

The Automobile Association would like to thank the following photographers, companies and picture libraries for their assistance in the preparation of this book.